Root Cellar

How to Start Your Root Cellar and Have the Freshest and Most Delicious Vegetables

(Discover Diy Hacks and Strategies on Food Storage and Creating Your Own Natural Refrigeration)

Dallas Moody

Published By **Ryan Princeton**

Dallas Moody

Root Cellar: How to Start Your Root Cellar and Have the Freshest and Most Delicious Vegetables (Discover Diy Hacks and Strategies on Food Storage and Creating Your Own Natural Refrigeration)

ISBN 978-1-998901-13-5

Legal & Disclaimer

The information contained in this ebook is not designed to replace or take the place of any form of medicine or professional medical advice. The information in this ebook has been provided for educational & entertainment purposes only.

The information contained in this book has been compiled from sources deemed reliable, and it is accurate to the best of the Author's knowledge; however, the Author cannot guarantee its accuracy and validity and cannot be held liable for any errors or omissions. Changes are periodically made to this book. You must consult your doctor or get professional medical advice before using any of the suggested remedies, techniques, or information in this book.

Table Of Contents

Chapter 1: Root Cellars - Our

Modern Natural Refrigerators

A root cellar can be described as a structure designed to store food. Root cellars are often built entirely underground. Underground construction is used to try to maintain cold temperatures that are usually underground.

The root cellar name is a mixture of the root crop word root and the underground cellar phrase cellar. This name derives its meaning from one of the main reasons root cellars exist: to store crops in underground or below-ground cellars in some cases.

Some root cellars are built outdoors, depending upon the area. This makes it easier for you to get to the items stored in your root cellar. Root cellars can save many different foods. Some foods can even be kept frozen for several weeks depending on the weather. Root basements are great for farmers looking to save their winter crops. They can then spread the crops evenly through that cold period. This is a great opportunity for winter produce to be freshened and enjoyed in a more convenient manner.

Root Cellars: The Past

Root cellars have been vital in sustaining fresh foods throughout history. In the past, cold-climate civilizations used ice to freeze their food. People who lived under tropical sun conditions dried their food in direct sunlight. These methods of food preservation made it possible to not have to harvest crops or hunt for food daily. People could enjoy their food longer.

Different cultures and tribes have their own ways of preserving their food. Some even bury it. Root cellars use this method to keep food underground, in cold earth. Root cellars date back to 40000 years ago, according to some sources.

The idea of walk-in food storage root vaults took off in 17th-century England.

This was also the time when the modern root-cellar was developed. The UK's residents took advantage of their cold climate by creating partially underground cellars that could preserve and store their food for long periods.

This skill of creating underground root cellars was carried from the UK over the Atlantic Ocean to North America. The first colonists established thousands of root gardens in the eastern part of Canada and America. Some of those root cellars are still in use today. These root cellars actually date back more than 200 years.

Root Cellars Today

Modern refrigerators have made root cellars practically non-existent. Modern refrigerators allow us to conveniently pick our food from our kitchens and store it for a long time. This is all done in the privacy of our homes and at surprisingly affordable prices. This is a luxury people used to not be able to experience.

Today, root cellars tend to be reserved for those who really value self-sufficiency. Most root cellars are built out of love and for personal satisfaction. Some people use root cellars to store food in bulk. This is an easy, but efficient way to store food. This is ideal for those who live at remote locations.

The cost of purchasing large freezers and keeping them running throughout winter can make it expensive for both homeowners and farmers. Some farmers store their crop for a few weeks. Every penny you save in electricity over extended periods of storage adds up. Root cellars may be a great money-saver.

Apart from farmers, root cellaring is also a subject of interest to homesteaders as well as DIY fanatics, gardeners, or organic farmers. Root cellars are gaining a lot of attention in recent years. This means that root cellaring is being enjoyed by more people than ever. There's a wonderful sense of accomplishment and purpose in growing and preserving your own foods.

The benefits of a root cellar

Root cellars are now considered an environmentally friendly method of storing produce and crops. This is the reason root cellars have become so popular. Farmers and supermarkets will have to make difficult decisions about how long they store large quantities. While freezer real property is valuable in supermarkets, the primary purpose of supermarkets is to store produce for a short time, it is not the supermarket's primary goal. Instead, supermarkets would stock many goods in an effort to move stock faster.

Both farmers and grocery shop owners are at risk of losing stock due freezer burn, transport damage and other technical issues. The sheer volume of produce that many farmers must manage over long periods is staggering, as I mentioned before. The farmer can incur increased expenses due to the amount of electricity stored over such long periods.

Farmer can end up paying more if they rent cold storage units off-site. This means that transport costs will increase for both the farmer and his personal vehicle to haul the goods to the storage area to reconcile stock.

Root cellars are an excellent solution to these problems. You can save a lot of money by just taking a few minutes to ensure your stock is healthy. This means farmers don't need to spend excessively on storage. This means that farmers can give more attention to ensuring that the produce is maintained.

Homeowners are increasingly turning to root cellars for food security, especially in the face of food shortages. Many places in the United Kingdom were forced to shut down stores and businesses due to severe weather. The perfect solution is to create a root cellar that can store food for weeks or even months.

Your kitchen freezer may not be able to hold enough food to last you several weeks. You will find root cellars useful for power outages in those areas with frequent bad weather. Root cellars won't last as long as food in new freezers.

Root Cellar Requirements

Root cellars may be built virtually anywhere. The area in which you dig it up and where it will be constructed is a key factor in its effectiveness. Some areas may not be as warm as you would expect. The other problem is that people often dig into places where underground water is present.

Any water seeping beneath the ground could result in a potential disaster. This can cause your cellar to become extremely damp, which can lead you to mold and other bacteria. This will help you to avoid flooding the area. But you never know what will happen.

Water is not the only issue you might face; however, you can avoid it. Before you can begin to construct root cellars, be sure to learn the 5 basic requirements.

* Address

* Humidity

* Lighting

* Shelving

* Ventilation

Location

Root cellars have many advantages. Most of them are underground. This is where the earth experiences consistently low temperatures. This temperature is dependent on the weather and location. If you live in an area that is subject to cold temperatures all year, it will not be difficult to get started.

Some locations have both extreme summer and winter temperatures. If you decide to build a root room in this area, it will likely be only suitable for winter usage because the root chamber will warm up the same way the surrounding environment warms up. There is still hope. Your root cellar could be used in the winter to store your veggies.

It is important that your location has good drainage. This means the area should be able quickly dry out after it has rained or dew. An area with too much humidity can lead to mold growth in your root cellar. You should choose a spot with sandy soil to build one.

Humidity

It is vital that vegetables are preserved in humid conditions. Root vegetables can live for approximately 6 to 12 month in a root cellar that is maintained at the correct temperature and humidity. Environments that have high levels of humidity are the best for vegetables and fruit.

This is why you need to be aware of the humidity levels in your root-cellar. If your root basement doesn't adjust for humidity, it will dry out and your vegetables may start shriveling. Some people do not have the luxury of living where it is naturally humid. These people will often resort to spray bottles to mist their root gardens. This is similar what you'd see in grocery shops.

But, if the spray bottle is too strong, it could cause the entire area to become saturated. This can create standing water puddles that could lead to mold growth. This is something you do not want. The temperature and humidity can be controlled if you have proper ventilation installed in your root cellar. A good example would be to close your vents in rainy and cold conditions.

Lighting

Because of limited electricity supply, many root cellar owners opt for natural light solutions. The problem with this approach to lighting is that food can easily become spoiled when exposed to direct sunlight. Light can alter the color of food and reduce its nutritional value. Vegetables such as potatoes will turn green. Sweet potatoes may even start to sprout unnecessarily.

Other than using a windows to get natural light, a window could be installed to act as a vent. To keep the light out, cover up any window that you have. Even if electricity is available to light the root cellar, it can still have an adverse effect on the food within the cellar for a long time.

In such cases, it is best not to leave the light on when you aren't in your root cellar. This simple change can make a significant difference in how your food is preserved. You can cover your food by using a sheet to decrease the light exposure if you spend time in the root basement.

Shelving and Storage

Even though shelving may not be technically necessary, it's essential, especially for large root basements. Shelving can be used to create organized storage, while still allowing for airflow. In the root cellar, you can install shelves at different heights so that you can store various items such as a pumpkin crate or potato crate. While the crate is rectangular, the pumpkin is square.

It wouldn't make sense to install shelves in small root cellars that are located below your kitchen. You can choose small containers to store your food. To store many types of vegetables, root cellars will use permanent bins.

You will be able keep large quantities or specific types of vegetables with permanent bins. Stackable boxes, on other hand, can be used to store different types of vegetables. It is a great way to organize your items for those who may need them. Stackable bins make a great portable solution, especially if you want to remove the food while it is still in there and move it to another location.

Ventilation

Root cellar ventilation is one of the most important aspects. Root cellars must have vents to allow fresh air and stale out. It is a common mistake to completely eliminate ventilation when building a roots cellar. It is essential to seal the room tight so that it doesn't lose any cold air via vents.

However, this misconception is incorrect as food can spoil in an air-shut pantry.

Some foods can release ethylene gas which can speed up the process of rotting and ripening. A root cellar with little ventilation can also quickly become very humid, which can lead bacteria and mold growth.

Vent screens are important when creating venting solutions for your root basement. Flies can be kept away by adding fly screens. Metal gates can control air flow and the galvanized pipes will keep it from rusting.

Chapter 2: Building Your Own Root Cellar

Because there are so many root cellar types, the actual process for building a root room varies from person to person. It is also dependent upon the specific location. The four-step building process would likely be the most common. This article will provide a breakdown and some tips on how to build a root cellar.

1. Digging the Hole

2. Designing a Floor

3. Time to Build

4. Complete the Inside

Digging the Hole

Although creating a hole along your home may seem straightforward, there are important factors and planning that you should consider before you start. These essential elements are crucial to planning.

You do not want to overlook them. These are some crucial tips that will help you find the perfect hole.

When digging down into the earth, the minimum required depth is 10ft. This is where you can find the most appropriate temperature for your locale. It is also where temperatures are most stable. If you feel that this temperature is not sufficient, you should lower it.

The location of the digging is critical to the survival of your root basement. If you dig next a large tree, you'll most likely end-up having to go through the root system. The problem with tree root is that even though they can be cut, they will still grow back. This means that if you create a root cellar where the roots once lived, then there are a good chance of tree roots growing back in your cellar. A plan should be in place to deal with any unforeseen problems, such digging into a stone.

Try to locate a spot that gets little sun during the day, when looking for a prime location near your house. This may be located directly behind your house, or it could be on the side depending upon the direction of your home. It is possible to use your home as a shade shelter, but you should be aware if there are any drainage problems or water issues that could lead to a root cellar being damaged. Root cellars can be made worse by water puddles.

Make sure you adhere to all local building codes and regulations if you're planning to build close by your home. A building permit may be required in some cases. But, if your root cellar is not too close to your home, you will not need one.

It is important to be cautious when digging in close proximity to your home. You can easily cause a retaining-wall to fall if you do not take care. This could also result in further damage to the home. As soil can often fall into the holes, you cannot always be exact. Be flexible, especially if you live near your home.

Designing the Floor

After digging, make sure the floor level is perfect. You will need to install shelving or other items in the cellar. An uneven floor can quickly become irritating. Some root cellars have no earth floors at all. This is an easy, economical and natural method of preparing your root canal.

Bare floors do a fantastic job of keeping cold out with minimal maintenance. But, you can still ruin your clothes and shoes by entering the cellar. This can cause a lot dust to build up, which could eventually cover your produce. Also, rats and other creatures will be able to easily burrow into your root basement through the bare flooring.

The floor's structural integrity is one of its most important issues. Although your floor may appear very solid, it can become increasingly unstable with time. This can cause cracks or gradual failure of your structure.

It is recommended to add insulation and protection on your floor. A mesh screen like hardware cloth is perfect to keep rats out. Place crushed stone or gravel on top of the mesh and flatten as much as possible. Assisting in the integrity of the cellar's structure and design will also be made easier by placing rectangular tiles at the corners.

This is a natural way to prepare the root cellar floor. All of the issues mentioned above are eliminated. Concrete can be further enhanced by being poured. Concrete can make great flooring because it keeps the cold in as well as gravel. Concrete is also great for keeping your root cellar secure, especially when you are using brick and mortar.

Time to Build

Now comes fun! It is now time to lay the bricks and concrete blocks. There is little to no difference in the durability of bricks or blocks. However most people prefer larger building blocks when creating underground structures, cellars, and other types of construction. This environment is more volatile, so the wider concrete blocks are better suited for stability.

You can build from scratch with bricks. It allows you to be more flexible and build each section one-by-one. You have the ability to completely customize your structure. This method is, however, more difficult and will require more support from regular builders.

Construction of the roof will require a lot assistance. This is one the most difficult parts of the construction process. Your roof must be constructed correctly if it is to cover your root basement. Your roof must be strong and durable to withstand all pressure and forces. While plywood is an option for roofing, you should consider using concrete and/or rebar to make your roof stronger.

Precast concrete structures can be a great option for those who aren't DIY-savvy. These can be constructed by hardware stores in the exact dimensions you need. You can also purchase new septic containers at your local hardware store. There are two problems with septic tank -

you will need to take out the door and you will have no choice but to accept the floor.

You can build concrete structures without needing floors. You can still build your own floor to suit your needs. The structure must be inserted quickly into the excavation. Once everything is in place you will need fill the gaps along the sides. The sides can be filled with crushed stone. This will aid drainage, especially when you cover all the areas with heavy duty polymer.

Complete the Inside

You will need shelving for food items like fruit and vegetables. Shelves are the best option as they can be organized to provide bins for specific types of produce. The shelves should be attached to the wall and the floor. It's easy to knock over a shelf full of food. Many people mount their shelves to the walls. Here's a warning: Rot can spread from walls onto shelves.

Wood shelves are great as they are not as susceptible to heat and cold as metal.

Metal shelving might be more durable but it can be hard to control the temperature. It's best for these to be accommodated.

It is best for your root cellar and outside to connect to an exhaust pipe. This will improve ventilation. Without proper ventilation arrangements, you could have problems when preserving food. An exhaust will help to remove some of the humidity. You should make sure that the exhaust has some kind of protective mesh to keep out insects and rodents. A thermometer and an hygrometer are both good tools to have in your root cellar.

As important as you might think, electricity is not so crucial. The root cellar food will thrive in darkness. Root cellars can thrive in humid, dark, and cold conditions. However you must be aware of where you are going as well where you store your vegetables. Root cellars will always require dark areas even during daylight.

To make sure that your roots cellar is well lit, it is important to invest in some lighting. There are many people who can do more with a flashlight than a flashlight. It is best to run electricity into the root cellar, especially if there is a convenient power outlet. This can be used more than for lighting. This can be used to circulate the air within your root cellar. If you have a long-term interest in spending time in your root cellar, a power outlet might be an option.

Basement Root Cellar

There are many homes in the world that have a basement, but it is not finished or unused. This area is ideal for creating a root basement as it won't require much construction and will remain cool. It will be right below you house. If you have a large basement you might be able to build walls around the corner and block off that section of the room. You can then turn the space into a root cellar.

You'll still need to block out those windows to keep the sunlight out. However, try to avoid being too close to any window. Windows can be very helpful for ventilation during times of high demand. You will still need to place piping and other ventilation options. Installing a sink in the same basement is a great idea. This will enable you to wash your vegetable right after taking them out the root cellar.

Hillside Cellars

Ground-up and hillside root cellars are both underground cellars. They are usually located in a large pile of soil. It almost looks like the cellar is situated on top of an actual hill. If you have small hills around your property, you may be able dig into the hill to create your cellar or place a septic system. Ground-up basements are root cellars which have lots of soil placed on top. Most traditional hillside root cells are made out stone or rock.

Hole in Ground Cellar

These are small root cellars which are usually found under the kitchen. Most often, the hole is just under a trapdoor. A large wooden box, or trash can, may be used to fill the hole. Old fridges and chest freezers work well here. This is the perfect solution for those who desire additional storage for their fruits and vegetables.

Many homes in areas affected by frequent bad weather, like snow, don't have root cellars. This is especially useful in times when entire neighborhoods are snowed-in. Instead of relying on a few fridges/freezers, you can make the most of the cold by creating a small root cellar below your kitchen floor.

Chapter 3: Tips For Storing Root

Cellar Food

To preserve food, it is important to manage your root garden properly. There are many storage options. But, it all depends on the layout of your root basement and what kind of food you want to store.

Even in hot conditions, garlic and onions can survive. You can store these vegetables on higher shelves. You can keep them in the kitchen for a while, if necessary, before you store them in the root cellar. It is easier to find spoiled onions quickly if they are kept on the upper shelves. You can then quickly remove any bad onions by doing this. Although it's fine to combine them all in one bag or sack, if one of the onions does spoil, you might not have enough time to save the others.

It is a good practice to keep potatoes closer the floor. This is where they are usually cooler and more moist. It is important to make sure your potatoes are protected from the light. You can make potatoes go green if they are exposed to light. Be sure to leave enough ventilation for your potatoes when you cover them.

Vegetables that are sensitive to moisture can be placed in containers or buckets. You can add sand, or sawdust, to increase the moisture. If you do decide to try this approach, it is important that you are alert as the sand can rapidly absorb moisture. This will accelerate the rot of your vegetables. Another method to keep your vegetables moist is to add leaves.

Separation

The best way to extend the shelf life is to separate vegetables from fruits. Some foods may not have the same preservative properties. Different food types will react differently depending on the storage conditions in your root cellar. Some food require cooling, while others need dry conditions.

The humidity level of a cellar will vary according to its height. This is why it's a good idea to have two hygrometers so you can measure the different levels of humidity from top and bottom. So that you can arrange your vegetables in the best places on your shelves and test the humidity levels in your cellar, take some time to do so.

One of the most important aspects about separating your fruit and vegetable that is stored within your root cellar is flavor transmission. Contrasting tastes can make your food taste bad. It is possible for fruit like mangoes, nectarine and apples to go bad if they are kept in the same food container as onions.

Ethylene is a gas found in most fruits and veggies. The rate atwhich the gas is released will vary between different fruits and veggies. Some foods are faster to ripen than others. It is possible for fast-ripening food items to prematurely ripen if they are placed in the same space.

You might also want to consider dividing up your cellar into several different divisions. This can help you divide your produce in accordance with temperature and humidity. Even more can be done by adding vents and insulation around each division. Even though this careful preparation might seem daunting, those who have kept food stored for at least 9 months have found that proper temperature control and humidity control has made a significant difference.

Graduated Storage

Graded storage is designed to help separate damaged produce from unharmed. This is because damage produce tends to deteriorate quicker than that which is not. Vegetables, fruits and other vegetables have a protective outer skin that protects them from damage. This allows them to maintain their freshness.

Fruits that lose some of their skin will begin to deteriorate.

This means that the deterioration of the fruit has started earlier that expected. In other words, the damaged fruit will ripen quicker than the unaffected fruit. This applies to almost all fruits and vegetables that may have been cut, dented, bruised or scratched. It is possible for damaged fruit to be mixed with undamaged, which could make the undamaged fruit deteriorate quicker than expected.

This is why it's so important to grade specific fruits. If you want to preserve your food for a long time, it won't make sense to put the same variety of fruit in the box. It's best for high-grade fruits to be kept in a separate bin from damaged. So you can see which fruit you need to use first, you can stack the damaged fruit on top of the high-grade ones.

Because fruit can begin to deteriorate from even small scratches and dents, it's important to treat your produce with the greatest care. Even if you have properly separated your fruit, mistreatment during storage could cause serious damage. If there are a few apples that get scuffed, you can spoil your entire batch.

Excessive ethylene gas should be avoided

Many fruits and veggies emit ethylene, a colorless gas. The size and composition of the food affects how much ethylene a particular fruit or vegetable emits. This is part decomposing gas. This is why some foods are riper and more easily discarded than others.

It is not wise to place large quantities of ethylene gas-releasing vegetables next to smaller ones. Extra ethylene gas can lead to a vegetable that releases less gas being able to decompose much faster than it would in normal circumstances. You must ensure that you keep these vegetables separate. Below are some of the affected vegetables and fruits by ethylene gas.

Food that produces excessive ethylene gas

* Apples

* Apricots

* Avocados

* Blueberries

* Bananas

* Cranberries

* Figs

* Grapes

* Guavas

* Green onion

* Honeydew

* Mangoes

* Melons

* Mushrooms

* Nectarines

* Peaches

* Pears

* Pineapple

* Plums

* Tomatoes

* Watermelon

List of food that can be affected by excess ethylene gas

* Broccoli

* Cabbage

* Carrots

* Cauliflower

* Chard

* Cucumbers

* Eggplant

* Green Beans

* Kiwi Fruit

* Leafy Greens

* Lettuce

* Parsley

* Peas

* Peppers

* Potatoes

* Potted Plants

* Squash

* Sweet Potatoes

Chapter 4: What Foods Can Be

Stored Inside Root Cellars?

Root cellars should be used for most food types, except fruit. There are many reasons you should keep vegetables in a roots cellar. A root cellar is a great place to store your summer produce so you can preserve it through winter. This will enable you to enjoy fresh, tasty vegetables throughout winter.

Each produce will need to be preserved in a different way. Each vegetable will need to be kept at certain temperatures to keep it fresher for longer periods of time. Make sure to analyze the root cellar thoroughly before you start to calculate the temperatures that were experienced in the various parts. It can be hard to accommodate all kinds and vegetables, especially if your vegetable harvest is small. You can avoid spoiling so much of your produce by doing as much research as you possibly can.

Below are some examples of vegetables and fruit that can be stored safely in a root cellar. You will get the best results from your preservation efforts if the following guidelines are followed. These statistics are only estimates. There are many variables that could affect the lifespan of a vegetable if it is kept in a root room. This is why you need to always pay attention to the items you have.

Potatoes for 4 to 6 Months

You can keep drained potatoes in a cool, dark area at about 45-60 degrees F. This is also known as the curing procedure, which aids in healing minor cuts. It also thickens and protects the skin. After curing potatoes, they should be stored between 40-45 degrees F. You could endanger their taste. Warmer temperatures could lead to sprouting.

Beans - 1 Year Plus

Once beans have been dried and are mature, they can be stored in your root cellar. Make sure to shell beans by yourself. Then, place them in an airtight bag. Beans can be stored in root cellars for a few years, provided they are properly handled.

Apples – 2-7 months

Use only mature, unblemished apple that you can wrap in a piece of paper. As mentioned in a previous chapter, if you have damaged apples you need to store them separately in a container. Undamaged apples will deteriorate much faster when they are bruised or damaged. Your wrapped apples should be kept in cardboard boxes or wooden apple cases.

Broccoli: 1 to 2 Weeks

Broccoli needs to be stored at 32F with high levels moisture. Place the broccoli in an airtight plastic bag. Keep away from any other vegetables or fruits that release ethylene gas. This colorless gas will drastically reduce the lifespan of broccoli.

Cabbage for 3 to 4 Months

Place your cabbage in separate storage boxes that can be shut up like garbage bags. You don't want the cabbage smell to get into your entire root cellar. It is possible for the smell to cause adverse effects on other vegetables and fruits. Wrap each cabbage tightly and place them on a shelf. It is important to keep the cabbages apart.

Pears – 2 to3 Months

Like apples, store only unaltered pears. Undamaged pears can spoil much faster than damaged ones. Pears can be stored at temperatures between 30 and 35 degrees F. You should wrap each pear individually in newspaper before storing them in cardboard or wooden boxes. Note that pears that have been stored in temperatures above 75 degrees F may turn browning on the inside, but retain their exterior.

Carrots - From 4 to 6 Months

Carrots can easily be kept wherever they are growing, just like many root crops. If you have the space and freedom to do this without worrying about pests or rodents, then it is worth considering leaving your carrots here. If you do store carrots in your root basement, be sure to remove the tops. They can cause water loss and can dry out the carrot. As it can reduce the carrot's lifespan, make sure that the top is removed. It is possible to extend carrots' life by layering them in a moist-sand box.

Turnips – 4 to6 Months

Storing turnips is very similar to caring for carrots. Turnips have a strong smell that can be smelt throughout your root cellar. This is why it is important to ensure that these plants are rooted as long a possible.

Garlic - 5-8 Months

Garlic must also go through a curing process for approximately 14 days after being picked. It is important to cure garlic in a well-ventilated location. Once the garlic has cured, you can remove the tops of the garlic bulbs and store them in mesh bags. Garlic should be stored in dry areas. Any sign of moisture can cause your garlic sprout.

Sweet potatoes - 4 to6 months

A maximum of 10 days is required for sweet potatoes. After the curing process is completed, sweet potato can be stored in a cool dry area at 60 F. If you aren't careful sweet potatoes can sprout.

Tomatoes, 4 to6 Months

Tomatoes may be stored in winter storage for as long as 6 months. Pick tomatoes before they become fully ripe. You can then store them in the refrigerator and watch them mature. You can get the best results by wrapping the tomatoes individually in newspaper. Then, store them in wooden cases at a temperature around 55 degrees F.

Leeks – 3 to4 Months

The same as carrots, you can also leave leeks mulched in your garden. You can also keep them in your root basement in a sealed container filled with sand. They should be kept upright in the soil.

Brussels Sprouts – 3 - 5 Weeks

It is possible pick out your Brussels Sprouts and to re-pot before you put them into your root cellar. You can still harvest them, but the shelf life of Brussels sprouts is short. This is why you need to be very careful about them.

Radishes -- 2 to3 Months

You can layer radishes on top of each other in a box with moist, sand-like material. It is important to be aware of the odors you leave behind. These can cause food poisoning.

Beets 3 to 5-Months

Similar to carrots. Dig up your beets. Cut off the greens. Keep your beets about 1 to 2-inches from the root. You can also place your beets inside a plastic container that is filled with moist soil. The beets should not touch eachother as this can cause them both to spoil.

Pumpkins – 5 to6 Months

Pumpkins must cure for at least ten working days before they can be stored. The stem should not be removed. This can cause the pumpkins to spoil. Same applies to squash.

It is important you note that there many factors that affect the time that fruit and vegetable will stay preserved. One of them is whether they are from early or later crops. Late maturing plants are better for storage in most cases.

For long-lasting produce, the storage conditions in your root basement are of paramount importance. The root cellar should be kept in medium-low temperatures. If the temperature is too high, your plants will suffer from a reduced lifespan. You must also consider how your vegetables are stored. The longer your produce lasts, the better. In root cellars, vegetables and fruits have been known to rot. This should be avoided.

Chapter 5: Planning Essentials

While root cellars may be seen as an expensive luxury today, they were vitally important in the past.

Root cellars can come in handy if done correctly. The consequences of losing your fridge contents or freezer contents in a power cut are devastating. But a well-stocked roots cellar ensures that you won't go hungry.

You can lower your utility costs by installing a root basement. You can store just as much in a decent basement as you would in a big refrigerator.

Root cellars offer more than storage; they can provide shelter from extreme weather conditions.

A root cellar, then, is a space that makes use of the earth's natural cooling, humidifying, or insulating properties to preserve food. However, root cellars must be able to maintain stable temperatures between 32-40°F and ventilation between 85-95% humidity.

Stable temperatures are required to stop microorganisms from growing in your food. Also, to slow down the speed at which ethylene gas is released. Both of these factors will reduce the amount of ethylene gas released and help you to preserve your food.

The humidity stops roots, vegetables and tubers drying out.

Planning includes deciding what kind of root room you want. Many people mistakenly believe that the root cellar can be dug next to the foundations. But, you run the risk that your foundations will be compromised and the cost of building something could be minimal.

The ideal distance between your house and the nearest tree is twenty feet. You can avoid damaging your foundations as well as avoiding any problems with groundwater.

Hillside is a great option for root cellars. Here, the root cellar has been dug into a hillside with the floor sloped towards drainage. It is possible to add drainage pipes in order to keep your root basement dry. Remember that PVC piping was not as common as drain pipes in the past. Instead, root cellars were designed and constructed properly.

If you are considering a pit-style underground, your pit should be square at one end and sloped at the other. This allows you to add steps above the slope.

Make sure you have holes in your garbage can - metal cans cannot breathe. Foods that aren't will spoil quickly.

Basic Tips

Different households have different eating habits. Root cellars' contents and design will vary based on their needs. Root cellars are great for storing root vegetables and tubers.

You may wonder why you shouldn't buy these vegetables when you are ready. You can buy them as often as you like, but make sure you are paying attention to the quality of the vegetables you purchase at the grocery store. They are often damaged or bruised, and some are already going bad. A root cellar is an option for people who have the space to grow their own vegetables, or are close to a farmer's market.

It is also a benefit to know that your food has not had pesticides or chemicals applied to it. You will also be able to rest assured that even in the worst of times, your food won't go bad.

These are the essential principles for planning and building a root-cellar that you will succeed.

* Talk to your local building department. It is not a good idea to get in trouble for violating any building regulations. If you are constructing a root cellar, your local building authority can inform you about any requirements. Before you can begin, you should follow all applicable codes or construction regulations.

* Prepare a plan -- Design your root basement to meet your food storage objectives and consider any disabilities. Consider a more accessible version of your root cellar if you are unable or unable to use ladders or stairs.

* Choose your root cellar size. It should be large enough to store all the food that you desire. It's no good to have a tiny root basement if you produce an entire acre of food. A small amount of food is enough to keep you from building a huge one. Take care when building underground. There are many potential dangers including structural failure, unwanted chemicals building up, caveins, and others. To create a death trap, you don't want it! It is important to remember that your underground structure will be weighed down by immense weight. It is essential to ensure that your design and construction are perfect. Make sure you design your cellar from ground up to make sure it is safe and sound.

* Pay attention to the location. This means you must take into account every aspect of your land. Some areas have high water tables and others have septic tanks. Either way, the root cellar could flood or fail. Also consider how far it is from your house. If the cellar is too far away, it won't make it easy to find vegetables to cook for dinner. Some people build root cellars beneath their garden sheds, which have access inside. Even if it snows a lot in winter, they can still reach the storage by simply removing the snow.

You don't want the soil to be rocky or with tree roots. You'll need to get rid of them, as they may grow again and cause damage to your cellar.

* Be aware of the critical aspects. Consider controlling temperature, drainage as well as ventilation when designing your home. All of these aspects are critical and will determine how long your food will keep in storage. Commonly, people build a root cellar according to the food they intend to

store. Consider these questions as you plan your project:

* Will my food need to remain in a warm and dry area, a moist but cool environment, or dry and cool environments?

* Does my food have to be ventilated to remove excess ethylene gas so that it doesn't start to rot or splinter?

Designing your root cellar with flexibility and the ability to change its climate according your storage needs is the best option. Remember that you might not have the same crops every year.

* The foundations -- The next step is to plan the foundations for your cellar. Dig down at least 10 feet. This will get you below the ground, where the temperature stabilizes. You may need to dig a little deeper if you have sandy soil or loamy soil.

* Lining the walls -- Consider using cinder blocks to line your walls. They are much cheaper, stronger, and easier to use. Make

sure your walls are built on the foundation. It will make them last longer.

* Plan your floor. While some people believe that a cement flooring is the best, gravel, dirt, and natural dirt are better options. This will retain moisture more efficiently than a concrete floor. The idea is to keep humidity high.

* What about the roof. Graded ceilings are better at keeping rain out. You can put a lot of snow and rain on the roof. This will add weight to your cellar foundations.

* Ventilation -- This important step in constructing your root basement will keep moisture out and prevent humidity from spoiling crops. Condensation, or excessive moisture, can lead to water running all over your crop, leading to spoilage and rot.

If you decide to transform an existing space or building, follow the same guidelines about location and make any necessary alterations to achieve your goals.

Maintaining Your Root Cellar

Root cellars can be quite easy to maintain. A thermometer or a hygrometer can be two of your most valuable investments. Your cellar must meet the following conditions:

* Humidity -- 90% to 95 percent

* Temperature -- 32 to 40 degrees Fahrenheit

* Ventilation -- Permanent and properly installed

It can be difficult to maintain a constant temperature. Most root cellars need to maintain a cool temperature by using soil temperatures. You may need to dig the cellar in a deeper hole depending on where you live. This is why it is important to research.

It is very simple to increase humidity levels. Simply leave some water bowls at the cellar. After that, you can experiment with humidity and determine the number of bowls needed to maintain the humidity at the ideal level. It is important to ensure that your root cellar remains dry. Water can attract bugs and other unwanted animals.

If humidity is low, adjust the size or angle of your ventilation to suit the winds. Screen your ventilation to prevent insects, dirt, and rain from entering your cellar.

Proper ventilation can prevent ethylene gases from building up, destroying or prematurely sprouting. Ethylene is smellless and is often associated to fruits like bananas, apples, and other citrus fruits.

Ventilation Techniques

Each root cellar has its own requirements for humidity and ventilation. It is vital to check the conditions inside your root basement before you begin construction. Also, make sure that your design allows you to make modifications later.

Ventilating your cellar by using two vents about 3-4 inches wide is probably the easiest. To maximize air circulation, the first vent should go near the top of the room while the second should go near the bottom.

The lighting conditions in your cellar are also important. A root cellar should always be dark. Too many lights can cause rotting, sprouting, and other problems. One light bulb should be kept in your root cellar. But it is best to only leave it on for a short time. Burlap can also be used for covering fruits and veggies. It allows light to pass through while still allowing adequate air circulation. Dark material is best for windows that are used as ventilation.

Organizing Your Space

It is important to consider what you will be storing in your space. If you only store one type of produce make sure that the temperature and humidity levels in the cellar are equal.

Make shelves with wood for storage and walls. Wood won't conduct heat or cold in the same way as metal and keeps temperatures steady. You should also ensure your storage options are at least two inches away from walls to prevent them drying out. You can store foods at different temperatures with shelving: colder at the bottom and warmer at the top.

Final, be sure to fill your produce with water and remember to check it each week. Don't throw away any produce that is not good. You will reap the benefits for your hard work.

The next chapter will walk you through the process of building a simple underground root-cell.

Chapter 6: How You Can Build A

Simple Root Cellar

Your garden is overflowing and you have plenty to eat. How will you dispose of the remainder?

Canning some of it can be tedious and costly. You could freeze it, but what if there's no space? Additionally, not all fruits/vegetables can be kept in the freezer or canned. You can build a root basement.

There are many options. Some have been covered previously. This section will guide you step-by step through building an underground root- cellar and a cellar-in-the basement.

Constructing an in-Ground Root Cellar

It takes dedication and time to build underground root cellars. A contractor who is skilled in building and has the appropriate equipment can help you.

First, you must choose the materials to build your root basement. Some options are:

* Natural stones

* Cinder/concrete block

* Cedar logs

* Tires loaded with dirt

Many people prefer cinder block because they are cheap and easy to get in any DIY store or builder's yard.

If you are open to trying something new and letting your creative side run wild, a fiberglass water tank might be the best option. These can be modified as needed and are more convenient than digging out walls and building new rooms. Make sure it's well ventilated, and there is at least one meter of soil around it.

Consider your flooring options for the underground root cellar. Concrete, flat stones, and packed earth floors with gravel are the most common choices. It's the most cost-effective option, but it can also be more controlled.

Step 1

The location of the root cellar is very important. It must be in an area where there is good drainage. Water should not run in. Consider the water table. A root cellar built in the ground cannot be constructed if it is above the watertable. The last thing you should do is ensure that your opening faces the north, this reduces exposure to the scorching sun. Keep in mind that your root cellar will require ventilation, temperature, and humidity.

Step Two

This hole is yours!

Depending on the size and complexity of your root cellar you might need a backhoe.

Step 3

Dig deeper to find the footings for the cellar, and then pour the concrete. To harden, you'll need to leave the concrete for at least twenty-four hours to forty-eight.

Step Four

After the concrete has set you can begin building walls. Take your time. It's a huge job. If you try to lay every brick in one go, it will be disastrous. Consider hiring someone to help if it is not something you can do well.

You must also make sure that your ventilation is installed at this stage. The PVC pipe should be 3 to 4-inches in diameter and be installed at the cellar's base to draw in the colder atmosphere. To vent the hot air, and ethylene gas, another one of the same dimensions should be installed at the top. Make sure your vent pipes are covered with breathable screens. This will ensure that the air can still flow but keeps pests out.

Begin to frame your entrance while you build the wall. A way to enter is necessary. Place the footings five brick rows higher than the door.

Step Five

It is time to build your roof. For the top, you could simply pour a slab of concrete. But this will cause condensation problems. The best option is to make an arched roofing. You will need to be a master carpenter or have someone do the job for your!).

To make a sturdy structure, you'll need 1/2-inch plywood. 2x4s will be required.

Start by creating your skeleton from 2x4s and plywood.

Next, add plywood to the roof.

It should be assembled on the cellar wall.

Put the plywood over the top and cover it with a tight sheet of plastic. After that, attach it to the roof.

Now, pour your concrete. It should be at least 6 inches thick. Unless you have a contractor, you may need to cut sections.

Now is the time for patience. It is important that the concrete be dried completely before you can remove any wooden forms from the interior. Allow it to cure for two to three hours before you attempt to remove it. It is also advisable to apply a waterproof sealant on top of the concrete.

Step Six

Next, build your stairs. You will need to use concrete for this task, but you could also build them with wood. Your root cellar is now complete.

Due to their ability to keep animals out of your root room and cool the air inside, it is recommended that you have two doors. A light or other type of light should be placed at the top of your stairs to allow you to see your way down.

You can also add gravel to the cellar floor if you don't want it to be filled with earth.

Organize your Cellar

Put wooden shelves up on your walls. These shelves aren't as efficient at transferring heat and cold, and they can help you regulate your indoor temperatures. It's easy to install a thermometer (hygrometer) and get started with stacking your food.

How to build a Barrel Root Cellar

This is a simple way to build root cellars. This book includes plans for both small and large types. First, the little one.

Materials

* A five-gallon trash or barrel

* A drill with a bit

* A shovel

* A hay bale

Step One

It is important to determine the location of your barrel. It should be in a sunny, north-facing location to ensure that your vegetables stay cool and get minimal light exposure. You could either use the natural hills or pile soil to six feet. These locations are perfect for building barrel root cellars.

You can dig your own barrel, but you must be careful to avoid water problems.

Step Two

Gather your supplies. Get your supplies.

Step Three

Get drilling. Air circulation is important because the earth regulates the humidity of a root cellar. Drill some holes in the barrel's bottom. You could either remove the entire bottom or cut it off.

Step Four

Dig the hole. This is straightforward--just make sure the hole is large enough for the barrel. After confirming the barrel's size, place the barrel into the hole. Fill in the gaps with earth and make sure that your barrel rises at least 2 inches above the ground.

Step Five

Fill it up. Make sure you don't mix fruits and vegetables. It might be best to separate the containers for different kinds of produce. You eliminate the possibility of ethylene gas. Don't wash your vegetables before placing them in. This can pull moisture out of the vegetables. Just dig them up and rub off any loose soil.

Step Six

Seal it. Secure the lid. You can use a whole bale to protect your vegetables from freezing.

50-gallon Barrel Root Cellar

This is a bigger version of the previous design. The way you use it depends on what you are storing.

Materials

* Large wooden barrels or steel drums

* Sawdust

* Burlap sack

* Straw or piles de dead leaves

* Rocks

* Wooden leaves

You can use the second method below if you have no apples.

Step One

Dig a trench in the ground that is about half the depth as the barrel/drum. It should only be buried halfway into soil. Pack the earth around the barrel.

Step Two

Use a steel drum or metal drum. You'll need sawdust between the fruit, the sides and the bottom of the barrel. Freezing metal will quickly kill your harvest.

Step Three

Fill the barrel full of your apples. Burlap sacks filled with straw or dead leaves can be used to cover the barrel.

Step Four

Dig a drainage ditch to surround the barrel. The drainage ditch should be about 6 inches long and extend around the outside of the piles of soil. To help it stay down, you can place some rocks over the bag.

To get apples out of a barrel, just remove the bag and grab what you need. Keep an eye out for bad fruit and dispose of it promptly.

For other vegetables

It is possible to use your barrel for other vegetables, but it is a slightly different method.

Step 1.

Place the barrel in a well-drained location and make a hole. The barrel will be laid on top of the earth and then tilted downwards. This will prevent any moisture from entering the barrel.

Step Two

To provide insulation, you can cover the hole in straw or leaves. Next, insert the barrel into the hole. To prevent your veggies from falling out, place a piece of wood over the top. Place the soil on top of the board to fix it.

Step Three

Top the barrel with soil and cover the sides. The top and side of the barrel should be covered in approximately 18 inches, tapering down to 3 to 4 inches at the bottom.

Step Four

To stop straw being blown by wind, cover the entire barrel with straw. You have two options. Either lay the boards directly on top or make a roof over the top.

This article has covered all three types, with a previous chapter giving you more inspiration. You are sure to find the design that fits your space and storage needs, no matter how large or small.

DIY Shelving Systems for Produce

Once you're happy with your root cellar, the next step is to make storage arrangements. While you can pile your veggies in, this is a recipe for disaster. As you can see from the above, not all fruits and veggies go together well. Some should never be stored in close proximity to others. Some need to be stored in colder environments, while others prefer temperatures that are a bit warmer. This chapter will show you how to organize your root basement. Before we start, here are some suggestions for making easy DIY storage shelving. There are three possibilities. You can adjust them to your own needs.

Slide-Out Shelving Systems

A slide-out shelving system allows you to easily store and reach your fruits and vegetable whenever you need it. These make excellent racks for curing fruit and vegetables, such as apples or potatoes, or for ripening pears prior to storing them in winter storage. This simple, slide-out rack eliminates the need for extra floor space in order to store all your items.

Materials

* Four pieces, each 2 x 2. Wood eight feet long

* 14 pieces of 1x3 wood measuring 8 feet long

* Seven pieces each of 1x2 wood measuring eight feet long

* Brad nails 1 1/4-inch and 2-inch

* Self-tappet screws 2 in

* PH-Screws (pocket holes screws) - 2 1/2 Inches

You must first cut the wood to desired lengths. This will make it easier for you to put everything together. This is how to cut the wood.

Frame for the Vegetable Rack Frame

* Legs - 4 pieces of 2x2, 41 1/2 inches long

* Slide Drawer Gliders

* -- 16 pieces 1 x 3, 23 1/2 inch long

* 2 pieces 2 x 2 41 inch long. You should trim both ends at 60 degrees.

* 4 pieces 2 x 2, 41" long. Cut at the longest points one end at 60° off square, the other at 30-degrees off square. Be sure to cut both ends in the opposite direction.

* Front & Back Supports -- 4 pieces 1 x3, 25 1/4 inches long

For the Drawers

* 14 pieces each of 1x2, 23 1/2 inches and 2/3 inch.

* 14 pieces (2 x 2), 20 1/2 inches in length

* 49 pieces each of 1x3, 23 1/2 inches, and 3 3/4 inches.

It is important to keep the pieces that go into the frame and the drawers separated. You don't want them mixed up.

Tools

Make sure to have all your tools at hand before you get started.

* Quality tape measures

* A speed square

* Pencils

* Safety glasses

* Protect your ears

* A drill

* A circular-shaped saw

* A brad nailer

* A sander

* Stainer & brush

How to make a vegetable rack

You can read the following tips to ensure that you have all the necessary information.

First and foremost, ensure that you take all the right safety precautions and wear protective clothing/goggles/gloves where needed.

Work on smooth, level surfaces. Be sure to buy straight boards. Bending or twisting wood will cause you problems and make your work less enjoyable.

Check your work after each step. If you don't, the finished project will not be square. It will be difficult to go back to correct any errors.

Before you screw in the screws, make sure to predrill all holes. This makes it easy to install the screws, and the wood is less likely to be split or damaged.

Apply glue to your finished nails. It will give the nail a stronger hold. Staining your vegetable rack with glue is advisable. Excess glue will make it more difficult to apply the stain.

Have fun and be safe while you work on this project. It's important to remember that even though it may cost you some money, having someone else help you with something will be far safer and more rewarding.

Instructions

Step One

Work from the top to the bottom, attaching your 23 1/2-inch pieces of plywood to the four-inch long pieces of wooden frame. The pieces should be level on both sides, and they should be spaced at 2 1/2" between them. This will create a gap of 5 inches from one end of the wood to the other. If you measure diagonals from top and bottom (opposite corners), they should equal 47 3/4 inches. By doing this, you can see if your build square.

The ends must be identical. Side rails work as drawer guides so they must be fixed squarely. Otherwise, the drawers may not work. The side rails are attachable with glue or 2-inch brad nails.

Step Two

The cross-braces are two pieces of 412-inch 2x2 wooden. These will be strong and secure the rack. You can attach them diagonally at the back of the rack. One will suffice unless your rack is larger. If that happens, you will need both. Use glue and 14-inch brad nails to attach these to the rack.

If you plan to use both, your center angles must be 30° off square. For this reason, you should use PH screw heads to join them.

Step Three

Add your front & back supports with the 25 1/2-inch pieces made of wood. Attach them using glue & 2-inch screws.

Step Four

Your trays will take some time to construct. Trays use 23 1/4-inch plywood for the fronts and a 20 1/2-inch for the sides. To ensure airflow, you should leave a 3/4 inch space between your slats (33.3/4 inches). The diagonals should measure 32 1/4 inches.

You should build the first one. Make sure it slides well before you begin to build the rest.

Step 5

Now, put your trays in and your rack's complete! You are almost done with the build. Now it is time finish it. First, make sure to add a little candle wax onto the drawer slides.

Finish by sanding the rack and filling in all the nail holes and screws with wood filler. Continue to apply as much filler as you need. After the filler has dried completely you can sand wood with 120-gritsandpaper. Please follow the wood grain direction. Next, vacuum it out to eliminate any debris, and wipe it clean using a damp cloth.

Staining the wood now is the best way to go.

Fill it with your favorite things and have fun!

Flexible Storage Multi-Purpose

A root cellar is a laborious project that you will not regret. Second-rate storage shelves can cause damage to your root cellar. It is possible to make storage flexible by recognizing that your harvest could change each year and the possibility of different produce every year. This project allows for flexible storage. There are bins, drawers and shelves. All of them ventilated to allow fresh airflow. This structure can also be customized to your specifications.

Materials

These quantities refer to the basic construction. If you wish to modify it according to your specifications, scale the materials accordingly.

* 3/4-inch plywood available in 4 x 8 sheets

* 1 x 2s pinewood

* 1 x 3s pinewood

* 1/2 inch plywood

* 1 x 10s pinewood

* Wood glue

* L brackets

* 1/4 -inch drywall screws

* 3d & 6d finishing nails

Instructions

Step 1

Split the large sheet plywood into strips. The length depends on the height and width of your root cellar. Two strips will be required for each shelf.

Spread wood glue over one strip's face, and then adhere the second strip. Attach them using drywall screws.

Step 2

A story stick* will be helpful to ensure equal spacing between the cleats at your shelf uprights. These will hold your shelf and should be 1 1/2" wide with 1 3/4 inches between them. This will allow room for bins and shelves to slide out.

The top of your story stick should be held to the topmost part of an upright. To extend the markings across the panel, use a framing or square of drywall. To ensure uniform spacing across the panel, use the story stick on both ends.

A story stick is one simple but powerful tool you can use for complex wood projects. It's a rod or board to check the repeating measurements. Gradually mark the stick with the pencil. This is used to make sure your measurements are correct. You can easily use the same stick for all your woodwork projects, by making marks with a pencil. How convenient!

Step Three

Cut the 1 x 2-inch wood using cleats that measure 16 inches. Use glue and drywall screws to attach them on the upright faces. Pilot holes are a good idea before drilling the screws. This helps to avoid splitting your wood.

Step Four

To attach your uprights in your root cellar to the walls, floor and ceiling, use L brackets and concrete anchors. They should be spaced 24 to 28ins apart.

The spacing between uprights determines bin, drawer,, and shelf dimensions.

Step Five

To use as your spacing guide, first find or create a spacer. You should use the same spacing between your slats as the spacer.

Make sure your ventilated shelves are well-ventilated. Your 1 x3 side supports should be cut to the length you need.

To ensure adequate air circulation the slats must be placed on top and 1/8 inches apart from the side supports. Use a framing tool to ensure the slats are straight and square to the supports. You can attach the slats to your supports with wood glue or 3D finishing nails.

Step Six

Now you can make the drawers. You can now cut plywood bases using 1/2-inch plywood. For oval finger grips, use a 1-inch spade bit to drill and a table saw to make straight edges.

Drawer box made from 1x4 should be narrow enough to allow plywood to extend 1 1/2 inch beyond the front and sides. Use glue and screws for assembly.

Spread glue on your frame. Then, put the plywood on top.

Step Seven

Use 1 x10 wood as the sides to build your bins. Cut the top and bottom edges so they are 19 inches long each. Cut 16-inch runners using 2 x 2, then attach them to the top with glue and screw. You should cut slats approximately 1 x 3. They should be 3 1/2 inches shorter than your uprights.

Flip the sides over and fix the slats onto the bottom, front, and back using screws or glue. Make sure that the gaps are equal by using a spacer.

It's one of most versatile and flexible storage solutions, great for all kinds of produce.

2 x 4- Basic Shelving

Organising a root-room is a simple task. Get everything off of the floor. It is best to organize your root cellar with shelves. While they might get cluttered, you can quickly organize everything and make it orderly.

You can buy shelves and not make them. However, there are some who feel that the work they put into their root cellar means that store-bought shelving would not be enough. However, it is usually more economical to build your shelving yourself. For example, a 48-inch-by-24-inch-by 72-inch unit might cost between $80 and $100. You can build one that is at least twice the size and for half the time.

Materials

Thirteen 2x4s, 8 foot long.

* Two sheets each of 23/32 OSB plywood, 4 x 8, (If this is impossible, use plywood).

* 3-inch screws--try to avoid drywall screws

* A saw

Instructions

Step 1

Measure and cut your OSB sheets first. The OSB sheets should first be cut in half, so you have four shelves measuring 2x8. There are a few reasons that you might want the store to cut your OSB sheets for you.

1. It might fit more easily in or onto your car

2. It's far simpler to unload and get into your root cellar.

3. Less sawdust

Now we will move onto the corner posts. Your 2 x 4s should be cut down to 6 feet. Each 2 x4 should be cut into 4 pieces of 21-inch length.

End result: Eight 2x4s with 21-inch length pieces of 2x4, 44 2x4s measuring 6-feet.

Step Two

Next, pre drill and pre screw. You will need a drilling template to make the attachments to the 2x4 pieces. Now you can pre-drill your holes and prepare for the screws to be inserted.

Step Three

This is why pre-drilling and cutting first is so simple.

Mark the points where the shelf supports are going to cross your corner posts. Use a tape measuring instrument or scrap wood to mark the shelf heights.

The corner posts can now be attached with the end brackets. They should all be 21 inches long. So the total width combined with the side brackets is 24 inch.

Now comes the tricky part. First, decide whether your shelf end brackets should be toward the outside or inside. If you plan to put them in, you will need some shelf pieces cut to slide in. However, if you want them to go outside, the shelves should be notch.

Place the end parts on their sides about eight feet apart. Then, place your top supporting piece across them. So you can accurately measure the distance. Next, attach the supports to the bottom support. Do the same with the middle supports.

Once the OSB is cut or nailed, you will need to be patient to get the shelves installed. If you need to notch it, cut the shelves slightly larger. It is possible to cut the shelves in half. But, depending on whether you have any sag, it may be necessary to add a center support.

Congratulations! Congratulations!

Chapter 7: 8 Best Methods To

Organize A Root Cellar

You have already built your root cellar, and made your storage shelves. It is now time to put it in storage. Many people will get overexcited at this stage and start to pile in their veggies without really thinking about it.

If this is you then stop right now!

A root cellar organizer requires planning and much thought. There are many foods that don't get along and there is no one food that likes the same temperature. Next you will learn how each section of your cellar should be organized. You created your root basement with its own temperature zones. These temperatures allow you to keep your food fresh for as much time as possible. Organization is key to ensuring that your food can be accessed quickly.

Method 1 - Use the Drawers

Some fruits and vegetables can be stored in drawers if you have a root cellar. First, drawers in the colder parts of your root-cellar can be used to store fruits. This is because they do better in colder conditions. When fruits are kept at high temperatures and humidity, they can easily rot. It is best to store fruits in cooler, dry conditions.

Higher humidity prevents vegetables from drying. In warmer parts of the root basement, drawers can be used to store carrots, broccoli, and other produce. These items will last longer if there is a higher humidity. Some vegetables such as spinach or cauliflower can be spritzed with water daily to keep them fresh in grocery stores.

Drawers are great for storing produce, but you must be careful not to mix vegetables and fruits. Because every food type has a specific temperature and humidity, storing them together could cause loss and even mold.

Method 2 - The Upper Shelves

You should use the upper shelves for fast food. This includes food that is ready to eat, leftovers and beverages. These shelves are great because they are visible from the eye and easy to reach. If you have a root cellar that is extremely high and the shelves above your eyes are too high, you may need to reconsider your decision and find shelves you can easily see.

Method 3 -- Middle Shelves

The root cellar's temperature should remain at or near the middle shelves. This is because foods that are sensitive to heat and need to be kept chilled but not spoiling quickly, must be kept in this area. These items include eggs, cream and soft cheeses as well as deli meats. These shelves will also allow you to store peppers and sweet potatoes as well as squash, sweet potato, and tomato varieties.

Method 4 - Lower Shelves

Below the floor is where the temperature is lowest. This is also the area where food spoilage can occur, such as chicken, fish, etc. This keeps juices and other liquids from falling onto other foods. There are many vegetables you can store, including potatoes, cabbage and cauliflower, dried beans as well as onions, parsnips and dried beans.

Method 5 – Keeping a Journal

It is important to keep a record of what you do when you first begin a root cellar. It will help you keep track of all the items in your storage, as well as where they are located in your cellar. This information can be added to your cellar journal

* The date.

* The item to be stored.

* Keep an eye on the amount in storage. You should update this as you take stuff out.

* Other important information about the food you consider to be important, including notes on storage methods,

whether it must be moved or stored in a different part, and so forth.

The same is true for all foods you may want to can.

Method 6 -- Keep similar foods together

This applies to all foods - root vegetables as well as fruits, canned products, jars and more. For example, all canned fruits, pie ingredients, etc. should be stored in one location and tomato-based canned food or bottled foods another. Beets and potatoes should be stored close together. Also, fruit should not be kept in the same area as vegetables. There are some exceptions. The reason is ethylene gas.

Method 7- Rotate Your Food

It is important to check your food regularly. If you use your journal regularly, you will be able see the dates on everything. It is important to rotate cans, bottled foods and cheeses to ensure you only use the oldest. In this way, your food doesn't go to waste. Fruits and vegetables must be checked regularly. Anything that looks bad should be removed immediately. If you notice that something is starting to spoil, but is still edible you should immediately remove it. You may also be able freeze what you save. It is best to throw out anything that looks like it has gone bad. You also need to check the vegetables and fruits around it. They should also wiped down. It is possible that a moldy fruit or vegetable may spread to others.

Method 8- Store in containers

A container or bag is another way to store your vegetables inside a root cellar. Plastic tubs are one of the most commonly used containers and bags. Fast food outlets, restaurants, and supermarkets often sell five-gallon or larger tubs. You will most likely throw them away. Although they can be used for multiple purposes, some of these containers will include lids. You can however extend their life by cutting some slots into the lid edge to make it fit onto the container. These are great for storing multiple fruits and vegetable, but it is important to cut air holes in either the bottom or sides to allow air to circulate.

The wooden pallets can be used as the second container. They provide air circulation and are perfect for standing squash and pumpkins. A series of pallets can be used to make crates. You can store large quantities in one place by stacking newspaper or straw on top of layers of vegetables.

You can also make burlap bags and feed bags. Feed bags can be made from woven plastic. They are lightweight and breathable so they are perfect for food storage. They work well with apples and cabbages.

Also, wooden crates and cardboard boxes are excellent storage options. Some can be filled up with sand and used for storage of carrots and other root veggies. Layer vegetables with sand and continue to build up until you reach top.

Top Storage Tip

This chapter offers some additional tips on storage, as well as general information to assist you in making your storage organization run more smoothly and increase your chances at success.

While storage is critical for success, there's more you can do. You will lose all the hard work you put into planning.

Manage the Climate

As you already know, climate is key in a root cellar. This includes temperature, humidity, ventilation, and temperature. The ideal temperature for most crops is between 32 and 40 degrees Fahrenheit, with humidity of 90 to 95 per cent. Others require higher temperatures of 50 to 60 degrees with humidity between 60 and 70%. Root cellars built with dirt floors will retain more humidity than those made with concrete floors. A humidifier can be used to increase the humidity or you can place water bowls on your floor.

Air the Cellar

Proper ventilation will help to keep odors at bay, prevent rotting, spoilage, and regulate temperature and humidity. Proper ventilation is essential to keep odors out, slow rotting and spoilage down, and ensure you have adequate outlet and inlet pipes.

Keeping Your Root Cellar Cool

These tips will ensure your root cellar is in the best possible climate.

* It is important to dig your root cellar a minimum of ten feet (3 m) down in order to achieve complete temperature stability.

* Not digging your root cellar near big trees. The roots can not only be hard to dig though, but they can also grow and crack the walls of your carefully dug root basement.

* As wood does not conduct heat/cold like other materials, it should be used as much as you can for storage.

* To ensure adequate air circulation, stand your bins or storage shelves at least 1 inch away from a wall.

* Use packed earth floors instead of concrete.

* Install a hygrometer/thermometer to monitor temperature, humidity.

* Ensure adequate ventilation.

One last tip: Get it done now

* Keep the lights on. If your root cellar has windows make sure they're shaded. You should keep lights off where possible as too much light can cause loss of quality. Some vegetables may start sprouting.

Root Cellar Ventilation with Ethylene Gaz

The most common mistake in designing or installing a root cellar is not providing adequate ventilation. While most people assume that food storage areas need to be kept at room temperature to keep them cold, this is actually the fastest way to let food spoil.

This is by no means a good thing. Some foods can emit a gas called ethylene. While you won't be able to smell it, it is the main reason for food over-ripening.

Excessive humidity can also lead to mildew and mold growth in areas that are not well ventilated.

You probably already know that your cellar should have two vents. One near the ceiling and one near to the floor. The bottom vent allows for colder air to come in while the top vents warm and stale air out.

You can get away with a 4-inch PVC pipes if your room is approximately six by eight feet. If your room is bigger, the pipes will need to grow. All ventilation pipes need to be covered in mesh so pests or animals cannot get in.

The book mentions ethylene gas several times. This shows how important the subject is.

Some fruits, like apples and pears, produce this gas as they ripen. This decreases the shelf life of any other produce. It can cause premature sprouting of mold, rotting shrinking yellowing and softening of skins.

To stop this phenomenon, produce-producing fruits and vegetables must be kept separate from others that can be affected. These foods are susceptible to excess ethylene gas.

* Apricots

* Apples

* Avocados

* Yellow bananas

* Cantaloupes

* Blueberries

* All citrus fruits with the exception of grapefruit

* Figs

* Cranberries

* Grapes

* Guavas

* Honeydew melons

* Green onions

* Ripe Kiwifruit

* Melons

* Mangoes

* Nectarines

* Mushrooms

* Papayas

* Okras

* Passion fruit

* Watermelon

* Tomatoes

* Persimmons

* Peppers

* Pears

* Quince

* Plantains

* Prunes

* Pineapple

* Plums

Here are some vegetables and fruits that could be affected by ethylene gas.

* Broccoli

* Asparagus

* Cabbage

* Brussels sprouts

* Cauliflower

* Carrots

* Cucumbers

* Chard

* Eggplant

* Escarole

* Endive

* Green beans

* Kiwifruit

* Lettuce

* Kale

* Florist greens

* Cut flowers

* Peas

* Parsley

* Peppers

* Romaine lettuce

* Sweet potatoes

* Watercress

* Potatoes

* Leafy leaves

* Yams

* Spinach

* Squash

* Potted plants

10 Last Tips to Store Your Harvest

* Keep it as late in season as possible to stock your roots cellar. Before you store it in the cellar, make sure to keep it cool.

* Some vegetables like winter squash, pumpkins, potatoes, or onions should be cured for several hours before being placed in storage. It is important to do this in warm temperatures as it helps the skin

harden. This will make them last longer in storage.

* Do NOT wash vegetables before placing them in storage. Your vegetables will retain their freshness longer, while wet vegetables can rot more easily. If you have top-leaf vegetables like carrots or beets then it is best to cut the foliage back to about 1 inch.

* Take care when handling your vegetables in the harvesting and storage process. Even the smallest touch can cause invisiblebruising. This can lead to decomposition early on and early rot.

* Turnips or cabbages should be kept separate from other foods as their odors may contaminate all food.

* Most fruit can breathe, particularly pears or apples. To slow down the release, ethylene gases should be contained in individual wraps of paper.

To ensure freshness, arrange your vegetables on their shelves/trays. Storing them together can increase heat and speed up the process of decomposition.

* Make sure you check your produce often and get rid any that is not working.

Chapter 8: Common Problems

Troubleshooting

While owning a root basement should be a fun experience, there are likely problems anywhere food is stored. Food storage can lead to problems such as mold, pests, and so on. This chapter discusses the worst problems and offers solutions.

Tips for Root Cellar Success

Rodents

You can find mice and rats anywhere food is available, even in root cellars. They must be prevented from entering your root cellar. To do this, block their access points. It is best to use metal wire mesh. You can place it wherever mice may access your storage. If mice are often found in your cellar, you might want to move your storage out of reach. Keep in mind that rodents love to climb, so if they have your food as their prize, they won't stop at anything. You will learn more about natural ways to repel rodents from your root cellar. For now, however, you can keep it clean. It is possible to put traps along the walls. However, these must be checked at a minimum of once per day. Dead rodents must also be removed from the walls.

Rot

Rot is another common problem found in root cellars. You may have heard that "one rotten apples spoils the barrel", and that is certainly true. But how can you stop it from happening to you? Although you cannot completely stop it, there are ways to minimize its chances of happening.

You should take extra care when picking your vegetables. Before you store your produce, be sure to sort it out. Take out anything that is bruised. Dropping something like an apple and potato will cause an invisible bruise. Set it aside. Your root cellar should contain only undamaged, blemish free foods. You can either use them immediately or keep them in another form, like freezing or canning.

* A common mistake is to wash root vegetables before you store them. It's tempting, but it's not worth the effort. Root vegetables retain their best quality when they are freshly pulled from the ground with all of their roots, stems and soil intact. To store them, you just need to lightly brush off any dirt. Washing vegetables removes moisture and causes them to decay.

* Make sure all canned or bottled foods have airtight containers. Sterilize containers and lids prior to canning or bottling any items.

* When storing your produce, place the largest at the back and the smallest at first. These produce are more susceptible to escaping quickly and should be used soon.

Check for condensation if you have a high humidity basement. You can see the signs of rot in produce if water is leaking from the ceiling. It is important to disinfect your cellar ceiling before you store food. This helps prevent water-borne diseases.

Your root cellar should be inspected regularly as a matter of principle. If foods begin to wither, rot, and show signs of decay, they should be removed immediately.

Insects

This seems to be an issue where nuts and grain are stored. Also, since there is food in your root room, you should never use insecticides. Your best option to keep insects out is to make sure your door fits tightly. Or, you can scatter bay leaf around. These are good for keeping insects away.

Sprouting Vegetables

If your roots seem to be sprouting, that is a sign something is wrong. This can usually be traced to one of these:

* Ethylenegas -- Seek out the best place to store your vegetables sprouting. What are other nearby vegetables and fruits that give off excess Ethylene? If so, it is best to move them. Also, make sure to inspect your ventilation system. Does it work properly? Is your ventilation system working properly? Have you put it in the right spot? If you can't answer all of them, then it is likely that something needs to be done in your cellar.

* Too warm -- Too high temperatures can lead to vegetables growing faster than they should. Once a plant has started to grow, it needs to be consumed as soon as possible. Your ventilation system should be checked again to stop sprouting.

* Too much light -- Are you letting the door open when visiting your root cellar? Are the windows well covered? Do you leave the light on for prolonged periods of time? Keep vegetables in the dark as much as possible to prevent them from growing again.

Frozen Produce

If your root cellar freezes, it means that the temperature is too low. Start by checking your thermometer. To raise the temperature below freezing, check it. You might also have lost some of your stored foods at this point. Most vegetables will rot and go mushy when frozen, making them ineligible for use. Check to see what vegetables are still frozen. If there are no vegetables at the bottom it means that your root cellar was not deep enough. There are no other options than to empty it and dig deep. It is important to remember that temperature stability is achieved around ten feet below the surface or three metres underground.

Produce Going Off Too Fast

You opened the door to your root basement and were struck by the smell. Your food is going off fast and the smell can be quite strong. So what is causing that? It's all about the climate within your root cellar. The most important factors are humidity, light, temperature and microbial development.

The most rapid cause of fresh food being lost is the damage done by microorganisms. This happens only when the conditions are right. These microorganisms require nutrients and moisture to grow and reproduce. It is easy to see why fruits and vegetables are so attractive.

Fresh food is more vulnerable to light than fresh food. Too much light will cause damage to the outer layers of vegetables and fruits. Photodegradation also refers to the discoloration of vegetables and fruits, as well as loss of flavor and nutrients.

Do not store vegetables or fruits in their original packaging. The lack of proper air circulation can lead to rapid decay. Your humidity levels should not be too high. If they are, water can pool on the produce, causing rot.

It is important to consider the temperature of your vegetables. You should keep in mind that different vegetables prefer temperatures to be cooler. Extremes in temperature can cause major problems. If the food gets too cold, it can freeze and create ice crystals. These can be discolored and sometimes cause a slimy texture.

It is vital to establish the right climate before you start food storage. Your thermometer, hygrometer, and/or thermometer can be used to determine temperature and humidity once your cellar is filled. It is a good idea to keep a record of your results so you can detect problems early.

Mold

When your root cellar works as it should, it will be cool throughout the entire year. Also, humidity levels will not change. There is one thing that can ruin root cellars. It doesn't matter if they are underground, in a garage or basement, under the porch or in a barrel in the ground. You may think you have sealed your basement properly but construction defects or insufficient maintenance can lead mold growth where you don't want it.

Mold growth inside a root cellar or attached to your home could have a negative effect on your ability to breathe. If mold forms within a cold storage area or in a cellar, it's usually because of condensation. This may be due in part to warmer air leaking into the space during the summer months.

Condensation happens when warm air meets cold surfaces in the cellar such as the roof and poorly insulated walls. This creates the ideal environment for mold to thrive. Mold can quickly spread quickly from your produce to the containers in which it is stored.

The best way to control humidity in your root basement is with air vents. This helps to control humidity levels and prevent mold growth. The air vents keep fresh air flowing through the cellar while keeping it dry.

Mold can also be found in food. Mold can be introduced to your cellar via the food you eat. It doesn't matter if your root-cell structure is functioning well. The mold can spread to other food sources and your root-cell structure.

If you are concerned about mold growing in your root canal, it is imperative that you take immediate action. Mold can quickly spread from your root cellar to other areas of your home if it's not dealt with immediately. Expert help may be required to remove mold and repair some damage.

You might ask, "What harm?"

First and most importantly, the possible damage it can cause to your health. Long-term exposure is more likely for people with allergies, weak immune system, or respiratory diseases. But, even those without underlying issues, this can still affect them. It can lead asthma, bronchitis or allergic reactions. Some common signs of mold exposure are:

* Sneezing

* Coughing

* Constantly fatigue

* Eye and throat irritation

* Headaches

* Skin rashes and irritation

* Nausea

* Breathing problems

* Nosebleeds

It is strongly advised that you seek immediate medical assistance if you experience any of the above symptoms.

It can also damage the structural integrity of your house, root cellar, and other structures. It can infest your walls, ceilings, cause fungus to grow on wooden structures and even lead to wet or dry rot. You could be facing costly structural repairs if you leave it untreated.

Many people assume that the arrival of winter will end the growth of mold in their cellar. But, in reality, this is incorrect. While temperatures below freezing can slow down and freeze mold growth, they do little to dry out the moldspores. Thus, mold lies dormant. Once temperatures warm up, it starts growing quickly and hard.

So you can't wait for winter to come and try to fix the problem. There are two options. If the mold is only beginning to grow in the root cellar, it can be removed by removing everything and washing the surfaces with diluted chlorine bleach. Another option is hydrogen peroxide diluted to a solution containing three to ten %, distilled water vinegar, baking soda, or borax. Do not wash off these solutions completely.

As an aside, mold can only be removed from concrete surfaces that are already covered by water. Concrete is made from water. If water is added to the surface to clean the mold, the water is drawn further into the structure. This brings with it the mold and bacteria, making the problem even worse.

If the mold is covering more than 10 feet or is on concrete surfaces, then professional help is your second choice. Mold specialists can use the correct products and identify the source to remove the mold and fix the damage. They can also address air circulation issues and help you prevent the problem again.

Prevention of mold in your Root Cellar

It comes back to proper ventilation. This may seem like a thousandth reminder. But it should show you how important they are in a root-cellular that succeeds.

Make sure there is enough ventilation. The outlet should be close to the top, and the inlet vent should lie near the bottom. Hot air rises and is expelled from the room through the outlet pipe. The proper ventilation and adequate air circulation will also help control humidity and optimize air quality.

Other than your ventilation system, make sure that your cellar does not have any air leaks. Warm air can escape through cracks in the walls or in the doors frames. Your cellar should be a minimum of ten foot below the ground. Your inlet pipes will only draw air at a temperature equal to outside. Ten feet down is the constant temperature. In order to stop mold from growing, it is essential that any flaws are fixed as soon as possible. It will also prevent your basement from becoming contaminated with mold.

How to keep Critters away

Mice, rats, or any other pest can get into most things. A simple invitation is enough to get them in.

These are some ways to make sure they don't get into your storage boxes.

* Avoid Excess Moisture

Rodents are not only dependent on food for survival, but also need water. Rodents are always looking for places to eat, and you need to make sure that your root cellar does not become too moist.

Additionally, it is a smart idea to keep food off of the ground. This will reduce the likelihood that rodents will find it. Sometimes rodents can get into your food if it is wet. You open up the floodgates to destruction by adding easily accessible food.

* Eliminate Food and Water Smells

The previous tip states that rats and mice are more sensitive to food and/or water than you. It is vital to keep your root basement clean, free from water, and free-from food smells. However, air circulation will improve the situation. Strong food smells may still get into the air. To reduce trace odors, other smells can be used, such as deterrent rodents.

Rats and mice are not only looking for food and water; they also want nesting material. You should leave piles full of newspaper, sawdust and other materials for them to find. If you have enough, the rodents might build their nests right in your cellar.

Also, mice and rats can be tipped off by dust and mildew to the fact the area is relatively undeveloped. This signals to them that the area is safe. They then start nesting and multiplying. Fast.

* Spearmint or peppermint can be used as deterrents

If you've ever tried to grow mint in your garden, then you already know how difficult it can be. Many people choose to plant mint in pots. Raccoons, mice, rats, and other rodents hate the mint smell because it irritates both their noses as well as their throats. That knowledge can lead to two things. The first is to plant mint around the perimeter of your root cellar if it's outside. It will quickly spread, filling the space and surrounding your cellar. Second, sprinkle some mint leaves into your cellar. Place a few leaves in your bins for food storage. They will not harm the produce or cause any damage.

You should change the leaves every other week. The smell will last long enough to repel rodents. It will also mask any food and water odors.

You can boil some mint leaves in warm water and place it in spray bottles. Spray the cellar with water regularly to keep it fresh and protected.

* Use Mothballs

They are very strong and can be quite unpleasant to smell, but that is what they are for. You can discourage rodents or snakes by placing mothballs inside the root cellar. They hate it so they will avoid it. This could be what keeps pests out of your cellar. You may find the smell overwhelming at first but you will eventually get used it. You have a pretty obvious choice.

You will notice a strong smell coming from the root cellar.

Although they won't eat your produce or vegetables, snakes do not like rats and mice. Therefore, if the rodents don't go away, the snakes won't go away.

* Take a cat or two

Most cats are excellent micers and will definitely help deter rodents from coming near your root cellar. Your root cellar should be open to cats. Rodents that attempt to enter the area will likely lose or be dissuaded. You can bring a few cats with you to your root cellar. If rodents are present, cats will get rid of them. Cats can tell if rodents have been present by smelling their scents and alerting you. You might also find moles or chipmunks in your root cellar.

* Don't Run Away

Don't back away if rats or mice invade your root cellar. This also applies to snakes. These creatures don't want to be surrounded by people and they prefer being alone. Make noise, be firm and they will never listen.

You should make sure to visit the root basement at least once a week even if it is not necessary. It can also be used as an excuse for checking your crops and doing some cleaning. Some critters may decide to move on permanently if you are there regularly. If you do decide to go in and check on things, be noisy. Make noise, move food bins around, or yell at hidden creatures to inform them that you are there.

* Set some traps

This is not a good idea for children or cats who want to get into the root cellar. Peanut butter works well for mouse or rat traps. Also, keep a few more traps around in case you find a rat in the cellar. A small spring trap can be modified by nail boards attached to the metal bars. This makes catching rodents of various sizes easier.

Place the traps near the cellar walls. Rodents often live here. Do not leave the traps unattended. Larger rodents might be able to run with them. Inspect your traps daily. You should dispose of any trapped animals immediately. If they are still alive, it's better to take them out of their misery now than to leave them to suffer for many years.

You can also use poison bait, although this could lead to cats eating poisoned rodents.

Finally, if you're looking for a more humane way to keep them away from your cellar, consider an ultrasonic repellent.

* Keep a handy Steel Rod or Wooden Pole

Never go into your cellar without a hoe. Why? Because you don't want your food to be contaminated by rats, mice, or snakes. Don't touch food stored inside bins. Instead, you should use a digging tool to pull out your vegetables. If you don't know what to do, poke around with a rod.

Rats can grow up to one foot and a-half in length depending on the circumstances. Therefore, make sure that your rod is at the minimum of two or three feet long.

* Hardware Cloth

Hardware cloth can be difficult for mice and rats to chew so wrap your bins in it and place it on top. However, it is important to not just touch the armor without checking. Mice will be able to see through your armor and get into your home.

Hardware cloth acts as an excellent layer of protection. This why many people cover their walls with it in order to prevent pests from entering. It's made from flexible mesh wire mesh and is very hard for rodents. People who have used it say they are extremely happy with their results.

* Lock it Down

It is essential to secure your root cellar to prevent pests getting in. Your door should be strong and well secured to prevent pests from entering your root cellar. However, ventilation must be maintained. Cover your ventilation pipes with hardware cloth to allow for airflow and to prevent any other substances from entering.

Inside your root cellar, store your produce in chew-proof bins. Although you may not have to worry about rats or mice eating your produce, plastic and wooden containers will work well. Rodents will even use chewed-up plastic to build their nests.

There are other options available. You might also consider cement, cinderblock and metal. Metal ammo container work great if you have access to them. You also have the option of welding or soldering metal together to make it your own. It doesn't matter what kind of ammo container you use, make sure it fits tightly and has a protective cover.

* Guinea Fowl

The much under-rated Guinea fowl is last. They are loud and can dominate any poultry. They are one among the best pest repellents.

The best way to keep rats, mice and other creatures out of your root- cellar is to have them removed from your property. This will be where the guinea fowl comes in. They are excellent hunters and will eat bugs, ticks, and other pests. They can also be a wonderful alarm system so adding some to your flock will increase your chances of keeping pests away.

All in all, controlling pests in a root basement is a hard job that requires an ongoing effort. It is worth the effort. If you fail to keep on top of it, all your hard labor will be lost.

Chapter 9: How Does A Root Cellar

Thrive?

There are many things that you should consider before building a root cellar. Perhaps the most important is to plan the storage conditions that you will use for your fruits, vegetables, and other items.

Every root cellar, regardless of its design, follows the same principles. It should remain cool and dark throughout the year and not freeze. So simple, right? You can make the most of any cool space, whether it's your garage or basement. You could also go the DIY route and build one yourself in your garden. But there are two things you need to be aware of. Artificial cooling is necessary for areas with mild winters. If you live in hot areas, like the tundra or the Arctic, you might need to add insulation.

A quick Internet search can provide tons of plans to help you build a root- cellar. It is important that you don't choose the first plan. All root cellars are unique so you make sure to select the one that best suits your needs. What your root cellar does well is determined by its size and form. How is this possible? Because your personal size and shape affect how you deal the humidity and temperature.

Basics of Root Cellaring

Root cellars must be provided with three conditions, humidity, ventilation and temperature. The more you can reach the ideal conditions, your root cellar will have greater success.

Humidity

Root cellars require humidity levels between 85-95 percent. This keeps your stored produce safe from drying out and shriveling. You have three options for achieving the right level of humidity in root cellar.

* A dirt-floor -- Dirt floors retain more moisture than concrete and stone floors. Imagine a root cellar built into the ground.

If that happens, your root cellar will be in the ground. The soil will keep it moist. Once the earth has been compacted, you should add gravel to cover it. This accomplishes two things. It keeps your feet cool when it gets damp, and also retains moisture. Spray some water (carefully) on gravel that has dried in the cellar. The water that evaporates quickly will cause the air to become moister and humidier.

* Adding water -- These are the alternatives to adding gravel or concrete. Water can be added to the floor by spraying lightly on it, spreading moist burlap bags across the vegetables (but make sure they don't get soaked wet), or placing a few cups of water on it. These steps are required during the fall season, when you put your produce in storage. Dug-in root cells will not need to be humidified, but basement root chambers will. In humid areas, you can store root vegetables covered in plastic bins to keep them moist and firm.

* Sawdust moss or sandy -- If your humidity drops below optimum levels, there are three options. You have options. This is especially helpful for carrots (parsnips, beets) and helps to reduce surface evaporation.

Factor in that warmer air absorbs less moisture than cooler air. Your environment will become somewhat unstable if the root cellar is too cold or damp. For example, if your ambient temperature is 34 degrees Fahrenheit, the root cellar can still absorb some moisture. However, the temperature of the air can drop by a couple degrees to become saturated. This is what we call the "dew point", where the air cannot hold more water. That water will then condense onto your ceiling, walls, fruits, and vegetables. You can ensure that your humidity levels remain consistent by purchasing a hygrometer. These are available at most hardware stores and garden centers.

Ventilation

Proper ventilation can be just as important than humidity. Ventilation is vital to maintain a cool temperature in the cellar. The air intake must be adjusted to reduce extra humidity. This will prevent condensation from ruining all your hardwork. When air flows efficiently, it eliminates the harmful ethylene gas found in fruits as well as other odors that could affect other vegetables and fruits' flavors.

Knowing how the air circulates in your root cellar is essential. Remember that hot air rises (lighter), and cold water falls (heavier). You need two things if your cellar is large or enclosed. An air intake system, and an outgoing air source. The intake should sit low in the room. This allows cool air to flow in from the outside. For warmer air to escape, the outlet should not be lower than the intake. To facilitate air circulation, it is a good idea to have the outlet & inlet on opposite sides.

You might find one outlet that is high enough to cool the warm air is sufficient if your storage area is too small. It is important to elevate produce from the ground at least 2 inches. This allows air circulation beneath it.

Temperature

Above all, it is important to think about temperature when building a root basement. Good root cellars can do two things. One, they borrow cold. Two, they keep cold. How do you borrow the cold? It is very simple. Just dig into the soil. The earth will keep a steady temperature at 52 degrees below frost. This is because deep earth temperatures are less likely to be affected below freezing temperatures. It provides more protection for your vegetables. If you don't wish to dig a root cellar into the soil, you have two options. A window or an exhaust tube can be used to borrow the cold. These options will let you have cold night air, but it should be turned off during high temperatures.

Keep your temperature at 32-40 degrees and you will have the perfect space for food storage. The root cellar can still serve as a storage place for root vegetables or apples, even if the temperature is between 40-50°F. A month can be used to keep peppers, tomatoes, eggplant, or both.

You can make use of the difference in temperature between the ceiling and floor by placing your fruits/vegetables according to their storage requirements.

It is important to get a good thermometer in order to monitor the temperatures of your root cellar.

Tips for keeping your Root Cellar cool

These are just a few tips that can create the best atmosphere.

* Root cellars should only be dug within ten feet (3 m) of the ground. This is where temperature stability will occur.

* Do not site a dug-in root cellar near large trees. You will find it hard to dig the roots. Also, eventually they will grow through your cellar walls.

* To store produce, you should use wooden shelves, bins, platforms, and bins.

Wood does not heat or conduct cold as well as metal. Therefore, plastic may become brittle.

* Your shelves should be at least 1 to 3 inches away from the walls. This promotes air circulation, which reduces the likelihood of mold growing.

* If your root cellar is located outside, you should use packed earth for flooring. In a basement cellar, concrete will work better and be more practical.

* Be sure to keep a thermometer (and a reading hygrometer) handy. They should be checked every day.

* You can use inlets or outlets to regulate heat/cold flow into and out from the root cellar.

More Information on Storage and Root Cellar Conditions

* Place any vegetables that are sensitive to moisture in individual bags. Perforated, sealed plastic containers are another option. Regular plastic containers should

be avoided. However, they are useful for some things.

* However, you can also create dry microclimates using sealed containers and materials that absorb moisture. A cup of rice packed in a paper bag will absorb air moisture, but the bag will keep the rice away form your vegetables.

* Begin planning for your root cellar storage prior to the beginning of the planting seasons. For long storage, choose varieties.

* You should not wash your veggies after you have harvested them. The cellar may have anti-microbial properties. Washing it off could be harmful.

* Make sure to do enough research. Some vegetables can only be stored if they have been cured. Other vegetables will keep longer if they are exposed to frost. It is important to do your research so that you can ensure the best shelf life possible for your produce.

Keep anything that is damaged or deteriorated out of reach. Take out any vegetables or fruits that have been cut, bruised or cut during harvest.

* Keep your storage clean every couple of weeks. If there are any problems, take it out immediately to ensure that it doesn't affect your harvest.

What a Root Cellar Can Do For You

You can enjoy fruits and vegetables outside of season if you have a root cellar. This can be achieved without the need to boil, can, or freeze any food.

Also, you don't need to confine yourself to carrots and potatoes. When you plan your root-room program carefully, you will be able to store all types of vegetables, nuts, fresh tomatoes and sweet potatoes.

Don't panic if you don't find the time to fill your root cellar with all of the produce you have grown. You can find in-season produce at farmer's markets or store vegetables in the fall.

Here are some of these foods, along with useful indications.

Food Temperature Humidity Shelf life

Apples 32°F 90 to 95% Two to seven Months, depending upon the variety

Dried Beans 50-60°F 60-70% One year

Beets 32° 90° to 95% for three to five months

Broccoli 32 degrees F90 - 95% One to 2 weeks

Brussels Sprouts 32 Degrees F 90 to 95% Three-to-five Weeks

Cabbage 32°F 90 to 95% Three-to-four months

Carrots 32°F 90 to 95% Four- to six-months

Garlic 50-60 Degrees F 60-70 % Five to Eight Months

Jerusalem Artichokes 32 degrees F90 - 95% One to Two months

Leeks 32° F 90 to 95% 3 to 4 Months

Onions 50-60°F 60-70% Five to eight Months

Parsnips 32 degrees 90 to 95% During the first two months

Pears 30 Degrees 90 to 95% Two to Three months

Potatoes 40° to 45°F 90° to 95% For four to six months

Pumpkins 50-60 Degrees F 60 to 70% For five to six months

Rutabagas 32 Degrees F 90 to 95% - Two to Four Months

Squash 50-60 Degrees F 60-70 % Four to six Months

Sweet Potatoes 55-60°F 60-60% F 60 to 70% Four to six weeks

Tomatillos 50-60°F 60- 70%

Tomatoes 50 to 60% F 60 to 70 % One to two months-old green tomatoes

For those varieties bred to be winter-ready, expect to keep them for at least four to six more months

Turnips 32 degreesF 90 to 95% Four- to six months

The following table gives you an idea about the temperatures and humidity levels where certain foods can be stored. The next chapter will go into greater detail about foods that you should store.

What to put in a Root Cellar

Here are some things to keep in mind when making a decision about what you will grow or buy to store in a root cellar.

* Which varieties of plants or products you are interested in buying

* If you are growing your own food, choose the right time for each harvest

* The proper conditions for the storage of each vegetable or fruit

All this will ensure that your food supplies are as fresh as possible and don't lose their nutritional value or taste. Most food can be stored in damp and cold environments. Other foods need to be stored at a cooler temperature. Below are some good storage choices and information on how to harvest, store, and preserve the produce.

Cold and Damp

All listed fruits, vegetables and other items must be kept at 32-40°F and 90-95% humidity.

Apples

All people will have different opinions about what apples store best. However the consensus is that newer varieties and heirloom varieties tend to be less stable than older varieties. Winter Banana, a variety that is not as common, is one exception. It is also known that sweet apple varieties don't last as long as those of tart varieties.

How to Store

1. Pick your apples -- Select unblemished, unbruised and fully ripe apples. Any cut or bruised apple can quickly spoil a whole box. The stems will last longer than the ones without, so make sure you keep them on their stems.

2. Protect your apple - If you store your apples for long periods, make sure they don't touch each other. Wrap each individual apple in newspaper. You should also know the source of the ink if you're using recycled papers. Even though most newspapers are soy-based and some contain metals and toxic chemicals, you do not want your apples coming in contact. Avoid glossy papers, such magazines and newspaper inserts. These papers are often printed using toxic ink and have less protection than regular newspapers. Paper towels, butcher or paper bags can be used. If you don't wish to wrap the apple in plastic, place them in boxes filled with straw, damp, clean sawdust or sand.

3. Pack your apples. Place the apples in layers inside a small/medium wooden or cardboard box. It is important to not bruise your apples. Do not place too many apples in one box.

Your apples should be checked for rot at least once every week. You can use any that are showing signs of decay or get rid of them.

Avoid placing apples or other vegetables near your fruit/vegetables. The ethylene gas in apples can cause other foods to quickly overripen and spoil.

Varieties

These are the best varieties for long-term storage

* Arkansas black

* Criterion

* Cameo

* Honeycrisp

* Fuji

* Northern Spy

* Newtown Pippin

* Rome Beauty

* Pink Lady

* Yates

* Winter Banana

Shelf Life

Depending on which variety, between 2 and 7 months.

Beets

You should harvest beets after the weather has dried for a few more days. The roots must measure approximately 2 inches in diameter. You will need to remove the greens from the beets.

Wash the beets in cold water. Place them in a plastic bag or wooden container containing damp sand, sawdust, and peatmoss. Keep your beets away from each other. Use a bucket. Cover it with the lid. This will retain moisture.

Make sure to check your beets from time to time and remove any that seem in danger.

Varieties

These varieties are perfect for long-term preservation:

* Long Season

* Boltardy

* Lutz Green Leaf

Shelf Life

Beets can store between three and six months.

Broccoli

Broccoli has a reputation for being a short-storage vegetable. You can store it correctly and make it last for at least two weeks.

Remove the stems from your broccoli. You can now store it in clear plastic bags or place it upside-down inside a cellar. You have two options: either hang it upside down in the cellar or store it in perforated plastic bags.

Varieties

These varieties are perfect for long-term preservation:

* Green Comet

* Greenbelt

* Marathon

* Legacy

* Waltham 29

Shelf Life

Most likely, between one and deux weeks.

Brussels Sprouts

Brussels sprouts are great for storage, regardless of whether you like them or not. For the best taste, wait for several frosts to pass before harvesting. If your cellar has enough room, carefully pick the plant out and place it into a container. Then, place it in your cellar. Continue harvesting. Or, hang it in your cellar by the roots. If you don't have enough space, you can harvest your sprouts in small bags.

Varieties

The following varieties are perfect for long-term storage

* Long Island Improved

* Jade Cross

Shelf Life

Between three- and five week.

Cabbage

Red cabbage varieties will keep longer than their green or blanche counterparts. And, red cabbage varieties that are late-ripened are better than those which were early.

Harvest your cabbages once the first frost has gone. Cut the leaves and pull the plant out of the ground. Store cabbages that have unblemished, solid heads

These should be stored in bins and outside pits. The cabbage smell will travel through your home and could have a negative impact on the taste of your apples, pears and celery. If you are unable to store them in the roots cellar, wrap each head in paper, and keep it on a shelf.

Varieties

The following varieties can be stored for long periods of time:

* Danish Ballhead

* Brunswick

* Red Acre

* Late flat Dutch

* Storage no 4

* Red Drumhead

Shelf Life

Depending on which variety, it can take up to three to four weeks.

Carrots

Carrots can be stored right where you grew them, provided you have no pest problems.

If you are looking to store them indoors, take them out of their season before they freeze. If you need to remove the tops, trim them as close to your carrot as possible. The carrot's nutrients will be depleted and the moisture will evaporate quickly.

Place the carrots inside a container with peat, soil, or moist sand.

Varieties

These varieties are perfect for long-term preservation:

* Danvers

* Kingston

* Chantenay

*

* Bolero

* Nigel

* Kurota Chantenay

* Royal Chantenay

* Red Core Chantenay

* St Valery

Shelf Life

Depending on the variety, storage conditions and other factors, they can be kept for between four and six weeks.

Jerusalem Artichokes

Jerusalem artichokes keep better in the soil than in root cellars. They will stay fresh for longer periods of time if the ground is not frozen. They should be left in the ground to protect them from freezing and frost damage. They will soon deteriorate in texture, color and flavor.

Dig them up, take off the tops and rake the soil to keep them in your root cellar. Keep them in plastic bags or containers filled with damp sand. They should not be stored where they can dry out or shrivel up.

Varieties

These varieties are perfect for long-term preservation:

* Fuseau (most common)

* Coris Borlton Haynes (less prevalent)

Shelf Life

It can stay in the ground for up to ten days, provided that it does not freeze. Stored in the root cellar, for up 10 days in plastic bag and up to one to 2 months in sand.

Leeks

Leeks are another vegetable which can be kept in the ground through the winter or until they get hard frost. Mulch your Leeks and keep them there until the frost. Dig them up while keeping their roots intact.

Fill a large container with soil or damp sandy sand and put the leeks inside.

Varieties

The following varieties are suitable for long-term preservation:

* Musselburgh

* Arena

* Elephant

* Nebraska

* Zermatt

Shelf Life

You can spend three to four more months in your cellar or all winter in your ground, provided you don't get frost.

Parsnips

Parsnips can also remain in the ground throughout the winter, much like carrots. Mulch them and harvest them when you need them. Parsnips will not tolerate freeze/thaw cycles. It is better to harvest parsnips when it is cold.

They can be lifted at the end, or just after, the first frost. Then, store in boxes filled with damp sand, peat, or sphagnum moss.

Varieties

The following varieties are suitable for long-term preservation:

* Hollow Crown

* All-America

* Offenham

Shelf Life

Between one- and two months.

Pears

Pears react very sensitively to temperature changes. Store them at the lower end of 29 to 31, degrees. The pears won't ripen at higher temperatures if they are kept for too long. Instead, they turn brown and mushy within, while the outside looks great.

The unblemished fruit, which are best stored with their stems on, should be kept in the same way as apples. Wrap each pear with newspaper or paper, and place it in cardboard boxes or wooden boxes that have a perforated inner lining. This allows for good air circulation while maintaining moisture levels.

Varieties

The following varieties are suitable for long-term preservation:

* D'anjou

* Comice

* Bosc

Shelf Life

Between two and three weeks

Potatoes

Potatoes are one of the best root vegetables to store in a root cellar--

unsurprisingly so, considering they were the original reason root cellars were built.

Wait until the foliage is gone before you place the potatoes back in the ground. Leave them there for another 2 weeks. This will cure the skin, and allow it to harden before storage. Sort your potatoes by hand.

For immediate use, put any damaged or bruised potatoes to one side. Avoid eating potatoes that have green spots. These are chemicals that can cause stomach or intestinal problems.

You need to grade potatoes by their size. They should not be washed. Now, let the potatoes dry in a cool place for 10 to 14 days.

Once this is complete, you can place the potatoes into containers, boxes, burlap sacks, or bins. Each layer of potatoes should be separated by shredded paper and the sides should have air holes.

Avoid storing potatoes near fruits that emitethylene. Don't allow temperatures to rise.

Varieties

Most varieties of late potatoes will last well (early and later varieties are not designed for storage). The following varieties are excellent for long-term, safe storage:

* All Blue

* Red Pontiac

* Kennebec

* Sangre

* Katahdin

* Yukon Gold

* Sebago

Shelf Life

Between four and six weeks

Rutabagas

Rutabagas are able to stay in the ground, just like root vegetables. To prevent ground from freezing, you can apply a mulch layer ten- to twelve inches thick. The mulch should extend 18 inches between each row. Even if snow falls a few feet, roots are protected. But they must all be harvested before spring. If not, new growth may start from the tops.

If you are unable or unwilling to leave them in their ground all winter, lift them and brush off the dirt. Twist the tops so they can be stored longer. These should not be washed. However, they should be completely dry before you place them in storage.

Sort through the roots. Any that are damaged must be thrown away.

Layer the good root in a wooden bag or bucket. The roots should always be placed in a container that is not completely sealed. This allows the moist air to circulate.

Varieties

These varieties are perfect for long-term preservation:

* Laurentian

* American Purple Top

Shelf Life

Depending on which variety, between two to six weeks.

Turnips

These should be treated exactly like carrots, and kept dry. Turnips, unlike carrots must be stored in an outdoors pit. Otherwise, the smell permeates other foods and can taint their flavors.

Varieties

These varieties are excellent for long-term preservation:

* Purple White Top Globe

* Navet des Vertus Marteau

Shelf Life

Between four and six weeks

Winter Radishes

Winter radishes may withstand temperatures down as low to 28 degrees outside. If they are heavily mulched, they can be left in their natural habitat. It is possible to store winter radishes in an outdoor garden pit or garbage cans.

If you want to store them inside a root cellar cut the tops off and leave one inch of stem. Next, place the roots in boxes or baskets that are layered with sphagnum Moss or sand.

Varieties

These varieties are perfect for long-term preservation:

* Chinese White

* Black Spanish

* Violet de Gournay

Shelf Life

Between two and three weeks

Cool and dry

All vegetables and fruits in this list should keep at 50-60 degrees Fahrenheit at 60-70 percent humidity.

Dried Beans

Once your beans have produced fruit, place the pods in a dry area. If the beans rattle in their pods, it is a sign that they are drying. You can then dig up the plant, and keep it covered somewhere warm for an additional one to two weeks. To verify that they are dry, press your thumb into the pods.

The beans can be shelled manually or beaten against a brick wall to release their contents. To remove the chaff, you can use a hairdryer or compressor to blow it away. Finally, place the beans in an enclosed container.

Beans can be weevil-prone so freeze drying them for a few more weeks before you store them. This is done by placing them in single layers on trays, and then letting them freeze for several more weeks.

Varieties

The following varieties are perfect for long-term storage

* Black Coco

* Adzuki

* Jacob's Cattle

* Brown Dutch

* Steuben

* Speckled Cranberry

* Yin Yang

* Repokeb ("Tiger's Eye")

Shelf Life

Maximum one year

Garlic

Garlic is one among the easiest vegetables to store. First wait until half of your leaves have started to die, turning yellow or dark brown, and then grab a bulb. If the heads are still intact, but not broken, you may harvest them. However, if the heads are still tight and loose, it is best to leave them for a while.

Remove the garlic from the ground and clean it. Handling garlic should be done with care. To ensure that the garlic does not get sunburned, dry it in a cool place. Let them sit for ten to 14 days.

After that, tie the leaves together. Next, remove the tops and store the bulbs inside a mesh bag. They should be kept dry as they will start sprouting and won't be good to eat.

Varieties

The following varieties are suitable for long-term preservation:

* Marbled Purple Stripe

* Chilean Gold

* Porcelain

* Mother-of Pearl

* Tipatilla

Hard neck varieties are more difficult to store than their soft-neck counterparts.

Shelf Life

Between five and 8 months

Onions

Lift the onions once the tops have turned brown and they begin to fall. Take them apart and lay them on paper, screen or hardware cloth. Let them remain somewhere cool, dark, well-ventilated, for ten to fourteen more days, or until their roots are dry and the skin turns white.

Keep the tops of onions off by leaving about an inch. Plastic containers and bags that are not breathable are best avoided as onions will sprout if they're not kept dry.

Varieties

The following varieties are suitable for long-term preservation:

* Brunswick

* Australian Brown

* Copra

* Red Burgundy

* Bronze d'Amposta

* Newburg

* Red Creole

* Norstar

* Red Weathersfield

* Stuttgarter

* Rossa di Milano

* Yellow of Parma

* Yellow Globe

Some sweet varieties do not keep well.

Shelf Life

Between five and 8 months

Pumpkins

Pumpkins should be harvested by the first frost. As this prevents them from getting spoiled, you should leave about an inch of stem.

You can leave them to cure for about 10 days. You can also leave them outside if your weather is good. Curing hardens your skins, which means they will last for longer. However, you shouldn't store stems with broken or damaged stems.

The pumpkins may then be stored in your root cellar. They can be as high as two to three inches deep.

Varieties

These varieties are excellent for long-term preservation:

* Winter Luxury

* Howdens

Shelf Life

Between five and six weeks

Squash

Squash should be stored in the same way that pumpkins are cured, except that of acorn squash.

Varieties

These varieties are perfect for long-term preservation:

* Delicata

* Crown Prince

* Hubbard True Green: Improved

* Golden Delicious Hubbard

* Waltham Butternut

* Uchiki Kuri

Shelf Life

Between four and six weeks

Sweet Potatoes

Sweet potatoes should only be harvested when the vines are gone, usually in late autumn. To make sure that the potatoes are safe for consumption, you should carefully dig them up and put any damaged ones to one side. Allow the potatoes to dry in the sun for 5-10 days.

After that time, you will be able to move them into the root basement by wrapping each tube in paper and putting them in ventilated containers or boxes.

Varieties

The following varieties are suitable for long-term preservation:

* Centennial

* Allgold

* Jewell

Shelf Life

Between four and six weeks

Tomatoes

There is no need to wait for your tomatoes on the vines to ripen. You can either choose to pick them green and let them ripen on the shelf, or to store them longer. Certain varieties of tomatoes are more durable than others, provided the right conditions exist.

If you plan to store green tomatoes in a container, lift the entire vine off the ground and hang them upside down in the cellar. You can also take the tomatoes out of the ground and wrap each one with paper. The tomatoes should be stored at 55 degrees in order to allow them time to ripen. Green tomatoes typically take 10-14 days to ripen depending on their ideal temperature.

Varieties

These varieties are excellent for long-term preservation:

* Eva Purple Ball

* Green Thumb

* Fried Green Hybrid

* Old Fashioned Garen Pach

* Reverend Morrow, Long Keeper

* Red Siberian

* Red October

* Winter Keeper

* Ruby Treasure

Shelf Life

Standard green tomatoes will last approximately one to two months. Long-term storage varieties may take up six months.

Easy DIY Root Cellar Alternatives

It is not possible for everyone to have a root- cellar. There are lots of ways to store your produce in a small area if you don't have the space to grow it. These easy and cheap ideas will prove useful.

Garbage Can Root Cellar

Materials:

* A metal garbage bin with a lid

* A waterproof coating--a sheet of plastic or tarp

* A shovel

* Some straw

Garbage container root cellars can be used to store root vegetables like potatoes, carrots and turnips. It is nothing other than a hole dug through the ground. The can is then buried. Your vegetables are kept inside. Here's how to do it.

First, select your site. Trash can root cellars need to be placed where water drains away from it.

Next, dig your hole. The garbage can should fit within the hole. But, make sure the top extends several inches beyond the soil.

Put the root vegetables in a bowl and cover with a lid

Placing the straw on top of garbage cans about one to one-anda-half feet thick will ensure that all parts are covered.

You can cover your vegetables with a tarpaulin or plastic sheet. It keeps the straw in one place.

If you open the can to remove vegetables, be sure to inspect the rest. You can remove any vegetables you find that are beginning or ending to rot. If you have one rotten veggie in your storage, it can cause damage to the entire thing.

If you don't intend on getting vegetables out frequently, make sure that you check the contents at the can at most once a week. Never leave the lid off for very long periods. The light can cause damage to vegetables stored in the refrigerator.

Bucket Root Cellar

Materials

* A 5-gallon plastic bag with a lid

* A drill

* A shovel

* Straw (optional)

Five-gallon containers make the perfect mini root cellar for onions, potatoes and other root vegetables.

First, remove the bucket's bottom using a sharp blade or another cutting tool.

Next, dig in enough ground to allow for the bucket while keeping its top flush with soil.

Fill the bucket up with vegetables and close the lid.

Place a layer of straw over your vegetables to insulate them from the cold. Cover with plastic if you need to.

You can store less vegetables in this bag, but it's still worth checking on them every now and again to ensure that they're not getting spoiled.

Freezer Root Cellar

Materials:

* An old chest/upright or refrigerator

* PVC pipes

* A shovel

* A tarpaulin or large piece of plastic sheet

The old freezer can still be used as a root cellar if it is being replaced. If freon gas remains, you may need to contact a specialist.

If you don't have a refrigerator, freezer or other repurposeable item, visit your nearest scrap yard to search for one.

Get rid of all the parts that are not working from the refrigerator or freezer. It is important to remove all mechanical components and strip the back of your refrigerator or freezer.

You now need to create holes in your freezer's back. This method works well if you have a small drill bit. Don't be alarmed if the drill damages the plastic backing. These holes allow air flow into the root chamber and are vital to the project's success. If you dig enough into the ground, the temperature will remain around 55°F. This will prevent your vegetables freeze over the winter.

Over the back, attach a layer if fine-meshed bugs netting to cover the holes. Although your freezer will be below ground, it is impossible to determine what kind of creepy crawlies they might have.

Punch holes in the top of the freezer and the bottom. This is for air circulation. It allows air to flow out through the holes at the back. You should be careful. The airflow will ensure that the cold air is not drawn in.

Insert pipes into the two holes. The depth of your root cellar in ground will determine the length of the pipes. You want them to reach two to three foot above the ground. Then attach vents to top. This will prevent dirt and other liquids from falling down the pipes into your root basement.

Now you're ready to dig your own hole. The size of your refrigerator or freezer will determine how large it is. A backhoe is used by some, although it requires a lot more digging. You may not have one. Take your time if digging your own trenches.

Make sure you line your hole with bricks, rocks, and make sure it is even. This will increase airflow.

You should carefully place your refrigerator or freezer into the ground. It is important to leave enough space so that the door can be opened, especially if you are placing it next to a building.

Fill the freezer with soil, leaving space around it. To make a box, place boards about a foot from the freezer. This will stop dirt being kicked into your freezer from opening it.

Some regions experience relatively mild winters. However, others experience harsher and colder winters. Insulating your roof will make it more comfortable. This decreases the freezing temperature and reduces the chance of it being blown over by cold winds.

Make sure your cover is large enough to fit over the top and heavy enough to keep it from getting too cold. This will stop the freezer getting too cold, potentially freezing everything.

You're now ready to add your vegetables to your freezer. You can layer them in. Keep your fruits that emit ethylene gas, such as apples, separate. This can be accomplished by placing the baskets into your refrigerator or freezer.

Always ensure you check all other items before you take anything from storage.

Everything you do will come with a learning curve. Here's one potential scenario. If you stuff your freezer full of fruits and vegetable, everything will be fine - until it gets cold. You then find that all of your vegetables have frozen solid when your cellar is opened. Some vegetables can still be salvaged but all your squashes or pumpkins are gone.

All that was required to make the project work from the beginning was to add a temperature detector. Simple sensor plugs can do the trick. These switches turn on lights when the temperature drops below a specified level. A halogen bulbs is sufficient. They will raise the temperature to stop everything freezing. Your final step is adding your temperature sensor.

Pallet Root Cellar

Materials

* Six high-quality wooden boxes

* A tarpaulin or thick plastic sheet

* A shovel

* Tools to lift the pallets

Pallets are a great way to store root vegetables and dried goods underground. This could cost you some extra if you can't get pallets cheaply.

Place six pallets together. If you're unable to locate any, go to a garbage collection point, furniture moving company, or builder's merchant. They will usually have them, but they might charge you extra.

Measure the pallets. The standard ones are generally four feet by Four feet.

Dig a hole several inches larger than your pallets. You should leave enough space for the top of the pallet to be six inches below the ground. If your pallets are 4 ft square, dig the hole at a minimum of 4 ft in depth and width.

Line the hole with a tarp or thick plastic sheet. Be sure to leave enough space for it to drape around the hole.

Place the first box at the bottom of your hole.

For the walls of your cellar's walls, place four more pallets on top of the bottom one. They will not support eachother at this stage because the pallets have the same dimensions.

Take two pieces of 4" x 2. These should be the exact same width as your pallets. Attach them to your pallets either at the ends or sides using thick, sturdy string/bailing twine/wire. This will prevent your pallets being thrown in.

Attach the pallets at their corners using string or wire. You will have a sturdy box.

As you stand inside the box, remove the plastic and fill in the spaces between the outside walls and the sides with loose dirt.

You will need to pack the dirt in and make sure that the box is properly rooted in the ground. Move around the box and tamp it down. Next, roll the plastic up to remove it from the bottom.

You can now place your food into the box. For food storage, you can use 30-gallon plastic bins. Once your food is stored, you can fill the box and then place the final pallet on top. Keep it cool inside by placing the rolled material on top.

You can attach hinges to the top pallet, or you can create shelves that you can put inside the box. This is a basic root-cellar. You can make yours as elaborate or small as you want.

Add at least three inches of newspaper to the top of your cellar and cover it with a lid. Cover it with a plastic sheet and weight it down with bricks or ricks.

This is all it takes to create a basic root basement for your food. If you pack your food carefully, it can be stored for months. The only thing this cellar is unable to withstand is severe floods. It is not a good idea to have a cellar if your land is always soggy, or if there is a high water table.

A Basement Cold Storage Area

Materials:

* Other pieces of wood

* Other tools

* Insulation

* Vents

You can make a cold room in one corner of a basement that is adequate size and within your budget. This is not an easy project. You'll need to research how the air will circulate.

Insulate a corner of the basement. The walls provide you with the cooling effect and insulation stops cool-air from circulating throughout the basement. A contractor with experience in this area of work can help you if your skills are lacking.

First, pick your corner. You want your space to be exposed as much as possible to the outside walls. One wall should be exposed to the north.

Install a pair approximately 4-inch dryer vents. This will result is a type of siphon. It allows you control the flow of air outside the insulated rooms. You should consider vents with internal screens and damper controls that are manual. They should be installed at least ten inches from each other, and properly caulked.

PVC piping and dryer pipes can be used to run ductwork from one vent towards the floor. This will ensure that cold air is directed downward. It will flow down through the vent to the floor. As the warm, humid air rises, it will exit the second vent. An exhaust fan, although optional, can be added to aid in the airflow.

Create your doorway and wall frames.

You can add insulation to your interior walls by using 2-inch-thick extruded polstyrene plywood boarding. This boarding can be used to add insulation to the interior walls. It is waterproof, cost-effective, flexible, and can take temperature swings in the afternoons and nights.

Secure the board using polyurethane adhesive--construction quality is best--making sure to apply it in a continuous line.

As they are not in need of insulation, exterior walls won't require it.

Put a vapor shield on the warm side of walls. Plastic works best. Then tap the seams.

For external walls, you can use drywall panels or drywall. Don't finish the interior walls.

To insulate the ceiling of your cold room's cold room, use another vapor barrier.

To ensure the best air circulation, plan how your shelving will be set up. Metal shelves suspended from the ceiling work well.

Finally, put your door up. It should be insulated and sealed with weather stripping at the base.

Now you are ready for stocking your cold room. Make sure to clean your cold room often. Dust and dirt can cause mold growth which can be dangerous for your produce.

A Zeer Pot

Materials

* A large, clay pot

* A small clay clay pot with an lid

* Duct tape

* Sand

The creation of zeerpots is both fascinating and enjoyable. These pots can keep food cool by absorbing water from the sand and two different-sized pots. These are very simple to make.

Get your supplies together and make sure your clay containers are big enough for all the food you need. If you do not have one large enough to begin with, you can make many pots. You have no limit on the size. The outer pot can be any size you wish, as long the inner pot is just a few inches smaller than the outer.

For instance, a Zeerpot with an outer measurement of 10 inches is required.

* One clay pot, 8" diameter

* 1 clay pot, 10 in.

* Insulation/soil

* Cotton, burlap

* A 12-inch potting container

* Silicone, Cork, or other type of watertight substance for the plug

First, place the larger pot onto a flat, stable surface. Once it has been constructed, it will be heavy. Therefore, it is important to place it exactly where it will be used. It's best to have natural air flowing through it, such as on a walkway between two buildings, or on your balcony or terrace. It is possible to use a table located next to an opened window in a pinch if there is a cross wind. Place it in a large potting plate.

The base of your clay pot must be sealed if it has a hole. You can use a rubber stopper or ducttape to prevent water from leaking. To seal the plug, cut it so it meets the pot's bottom. The best pots are those that are solid and have no holes.

Add soil, vermiculite and sand to the bottom. The depth of your pot will depend on its size. However, you should ensure that the tops of both pots are even. This will allow for space for the next steps.

Place the smaller container in the middle of the larger pot. Level the tops. If you look from the top, it should look similar to the bullseye on an dartboard - an inner ring plus an outer ring with an even gap between them.

Note:

If the bottom of your smaller pot has a crack, you can cover the entire pot with plastic to make a waterproof barrier. Be aware that this might slightly alter your evaporative or insulating properties.

You can now add more insulating material. Be sure to evenly pour it between the inner pot and the outer one. Be careful not to spill any in the inner or outer pot.

If you see water in the inner pan at any stage during these steps, you should start over and seal the pot completely. It must be cool and dry. Water from the bottom can cause mold growth.

Use a funnel for transferring your insulation material to a larger pot.

Now it's time to start adding water. Slowly, allow the material to settle and then add insulation as required. Once the material is saturated, you can add small rocks or pebbles to it. These aren't for decorative purposes. The stones help ensure the insulation is evenly distributed when water is poured over them.

Filtration is required for water collected from streams, lakes or rivers. It could lead to food contamination as you don't know what is in the water.

Make sure to check the pot for leakages and then use silicone to plug them. The potting pan will catch any water that dries out of the pot, as well as the surface on which it is placed.

Now, you can add your food. Do not rush. Pots need to cool before food can be added. You can use the pot as a stand for your garden. Then, you can start to preserve it by adding the food small amounts each week. Zeer pots are great for tomatoes and carrots, as they can last up to three weeks.

Once you've put your food in, cover the pit. You have a few options. You will need a lid to cover the inner pot. A clay lid or an old slow cooker lid are both options. It is important to measure this before you start.

A substitute is to take enough cotton, cheesecloth and burlap to cover the pot. Do not use synthetics, blends, or polyester.

Soak the cloth with water, then wring it to remove any excess moisture. The cloth should be placed over the pot. Secure it if there are high winds. Use twine and rope, elastic bands or other materials as needed. As you add layers, be sure to keep the air flowing up to the top. Too much material could stop it. Pests are also prevented from getting in your pot by having more layers.

The cloth will need to be replaced for wet items as it dries. If you used multiple layers, remove one of them, soak it again, then place it at the base of the pile. This rotation prevents mold and mildew development because the layers are open to the air.

You should monitor your Zeerpot, then refill it when needed. Put a piece of tubing inside the insulating coating to keep track of the water level. You will be able to see the water level in the pot and know when it requires topping up.

Cautions

A Zeerpot is great at keeping food cool, but cannot be used in place of a freezer. Zeer pots can be used to freeze frozen food. This will take much longer than if it is left out on its own.

These pots must have moisture and adequate airflow to function well. If there isn't sufficient airflow, the pot won't cool down well. Evaporation won't work if your clothes don't dry out. Consider where the pot is situated, whether there is shade, temperature, and humidity.

Fill your Zeer Pot halfway with dampened sand, if you are using it to store root vegetable or scallions. To keep your vegetables fresher for longer, you can place them in the inner pot. Only the root parts of scallions can be buried.

Some things to keep in mind:

The minerals will build up over time. This can be removed from the pot's outer layer by using a sponge or some lemon juice.

To chill, the pot needs to be cooled by wind. The pot will stay chilled if it has a steady breeze or is fanned.

The pot won't perform as well when the humidity outside is high. So, make sure it's kept in a cool, ventilated area.

Last but not least, Zeer pots can go through at most two gallons of water per days in dry, warm, breezy weather. Instead of wasting water, take the clean water and save it for later. Alternativly, collect rainwater.

Construct a Spring House

Materials:

* Assorted wood-2"x4

* Other tools

* Create a small stream in your garden

* Cinder blocks

* A backhoe

* A shovel

* A measuring device

* Hammer and nails

* Stone

* Cement

* Gravel

* Tin roof

* Windows

* A door

* Storm pipe

* A level

You must have running water to make this work. Spring houses can be a beautiful, traditional way to store food.

Your structure should be situated near a stream or creek. If you are looking for the ideal spot, build your springhouse into the side of a hill with walls made from earth. You won't be able to do this, so make sure you are level and not too far from the water. Avoid areas with roots or rocks. It's important to redirect water from the source to the house through which it can be returned to the spring.

The spring's depth should be measured at various locations. This will give you an idea of the depth that your trench should go through the house. Don't forget that water will always find its height, so ensure the trench is approximately the same depth as the spring. This will allow water to flow through the structure easily.

Next, choose the length of your spring house. This allows you to work out the location where the spring will be diverted. The diversion point should only be a few ft from the walls.